Praise for *The Fourth Branch of Government*

"Having built my career on data management, I'd like to think I can recognize valuable information when I see it—and I *definitely* see it in *The Fourth Branch*. As I read this provocative book, my preconceived ideas and assumptions about how America's government *currently* works, versus how it *could* and *should* work, were challenged. I found myself agreeing with some of the authors' ideas and disagreeing with others, which I suspect Trammell and Terrell would be happy to hear. After all, if "we the people" really do want to take a more active hand in shaping and updating our democracy, Step One has to be a meaningful dialogue about what's wrong, what's right, and where we go from here. *The Fourth Branch* will help us kick off that discussion."

—Dr. Peter Aiken, Associate Professor of Information Systems, Virginia Commonwealth University (VCU); founding director, Data Blueprint/Institute for Data Research

"Between a crumbling middle class, the erosion of the Constitution, and the rise of anti-democratic forces, it's little wonder that many Americans feel a need to do *something*. *The Fourth Branch of Government: We the People*, suggests a path toward a more functional democracy. The authors would be the first to admit that they don't have all the answers, but they present a creative framework both for respecting the Founders and a democracy that works effectively in the 21ˢᵗ century. Among other suggestions, they would prune some outworn features of our system and replace them with novel mechanisms for greater citizen participation. Highly recommended for those who want to see power return to the people."

—Mike Lofgren, author of *The Deep State: The Fall of the Constitution and the Rise of a Shadow Government*

# The Fourth Branch of Government

*We the People*

# The Fourth Branch of Government

*We the People*

By Jack Trammell, PhD and Guy Terrell, MS, PMP

❋ *Brandylane*

www.brandylanepublishers.com

ISBN: 978-1-9399307-4-3
Library of Congress Control Number: 2016945334

Printed in the United States

Published by
Brandylane Publishers, Inc.

## Dedication/Acknowledgement

Any book-length project involves innumerable collaborations and other forms of help that should never go without notice and proper gratitude; this project was no exception.

Our primary debt, however, is to the Founders who bequeathed us all the tools necessary to make changes and updates to our democracy. It is our obligation to recognize and utilize them.

In addition, both authors would like to acknowledge the support of friends and family (you know who you are), without which this project would not have been born and then continued to bear fruit. Special thanks are due to Randolph-Macon College, the staff at historic Scotchtown, our video crew (Brian and Cliff), and innumerable non-profit organizations that share the same mission and have forwarded our cause, as well as their own. Bobbi Linkemer graciously provided us a roadmap to use with all the stops along the way given. The staff of Brandylane Publishers also deserves thanks, especially for enabling the book to come out in the midst of a campaign season (as we intended).

This project is not concluding with the publication of the book— that is just the beginning, and we thank you for embarking on the journey.

Jack and Guy
April, 2016

# Table of Contents

# Preface

Nothing will open your eyes to the current state of basic democracy as much as running for office. I had the privilege of running for Congress in 2014 in the Virginia seventh district (a seat held by Eric Cantor until 2014.) The experience transformed my beliefs about democracy in America. Although aspects of it could arguably make one more cynical about politics and government, overall it reenergized me and stimulated my thinking. The average voter does not have an immediate incentive to ask if our democracy works as it was intended or, more importantly, if it operates at the level it could achieve. Even politicians, as I discovered, busy with raising money and promoting a platform, don't always have the luxury to ask if this is the way our system should really be operating.

Out of that experience, I now believe our democracy is very much overdue for changes to improve it and keep it healthy in the coming centuries. Many of the practices and traditions that we follow come from a time that had no mass transportation, no electronic communication, and no clear sense that the electorate would be as diverse and as large as it is now. Many of our fundamental concepts of the operation of governance are sorely out of date, and in some cases, if not downright unfair, biased in favor of some portions of the electorate over others.

Our democracy needs a new installation, just like our ubiquitous computers periodically need to update their hardware and software. What shape and form those updates take drove the creation of this book. We need to have a grand, national conversation about e-voting, expanding Congress, redefining congressional roles, and expanding the capacity of every citizen to participate at some level in the creation of laws, an old idea the Founding Fathers had in the backs of their minds from knowledge of early Greek democracy. Democracy, when achieving its highest ideals, encourages a positive but critical and empirical dialogue about what makes sense and best represents everyone's best interests.

Having finished writing this book, I've come to believe that we need to start a movement to make this happen. I learned during the campaign that the power of numbers is not something to take lightly. There is a mathematics of engaged voters, and when a small group gains support and promotes good ideas, and then grows, change takes place. That process is happening, even as you read this book. The Fourth Branch of government to some extent already exists—in the organization and dissatisfaction residing within current elected leaders, grassroots organizations, and every single individual voter.

This book is just a beginning. Our Founding Fathers encouraged us to think of new frontiers and new possibilities for all citizens. I am not the first person to point to something that needs to be changed. The framework we propose is new. Change is the air America breathes. It is our hope you'll discover a new vision of the promise of America that can never die as you read this book.

— Jack Trammell

# INTRODUCTION

All of the great movements and advances in civilization have begun with an individual or group of individuals. Whether through art, music, technology, or politics, change occurs because first someone has an idea and lays out the application of the idea with a proof or a hope that it will work. We have tried to do that here. Alan Turing proved that a computer could work with an academic paper in 1936. It took a long, long time to finally get to the smart phone, requiring many other innovations and prototypes along the way. But the idea behind smart-phone technology began almost one hundred years ago.

The idea behind our unique democracy began even longer ago. Today, our democracy is quite different, and arguably in need of an update. The challenge is that everyone has very different ideas about how to facilitate that update.

This book cannot meet every expectation of every ideology and belief system, and that is not its intention. Instead, we are opening the door to seek new ways to improve the framework we use to govern ourselves in a twenty-first-century democracy. It will require changes to the Constitution that our founders planned for in general terms, which we believe is long overdue in 2016 with specific amendments and revisions. We simply must improve the way we make and manage laws, and the way that we facilitate democratic participation, with improved governance, or the well-being of our nation will continue to suffer.

This book tries to be bipartisan but sometimes we will inevitably fail and come down on one side or the other of an issue—although we are convinced of the need for the Fourth Branch, we are also citizens in the same system that we know needs change, and we have been influenced by it. We ask for your forbearance to look beyond the specifics of any given problem and instead to focus on the means or structures that can lead to change regardless of the partisan line on any given issue. Let us begin a journey together to improve our nation, a journey that focuses on our constitutional tools, and not on our political differences.

The Democratic and Republican parties did not exist as we know them when our founders created the Constitution. They envisioned a growing America that might have many types and varieties of futures and quite diverse needs. They created a framework that preserved the most important elements of the New Republic: individual freedoms, separations of power, rights to vote, respect for local authority—but they also included tools to update the Constitution and to meet as a nation to address our challenges.

Many people have written, spoken, and advocated for elements of what this book argues for. This book makes that argument more coherent and inclusive, and more accessible to every voter. The Fourth Branch is not just a book—it is a movement that has been building for quite some time in various forums, but lacking a central focus. This is the meta-movement that encompasses many efforts already under way—such as "your vote matters," or "make voting more accessible," or the League of Women Voters—and unites them to a common purpose: making our democracy effective in the new century and beyond.

Change is never easy, as the old phrase goes, but like the early suffragettes we have tools and technology, and combined with core beliefs, we are envisioning how our democracy can function better. Our founders wanted this for us. It was a gift, but one that we seldom use to its maximum utility. In our complicated times, we need every bit of innovation we can draw upon.

A disruptive technology never comes about as a singular event; it comes instead through a series of disruptions, or difficult conversations, which together begin to shape an outcome. Although change isn't easy, we believe that starting and continuing the conversation is quite practical. This book is that conversation, and we ask you to join us in it.

In the first three chapters, we discuss congressional dysfunction and the growing distance that voters feel from the actual decision-making and locus of power. In Chapters 4 and 5, we advocate for e-voting. Chapter 6 suggests retiring the electoral college. Chapters 7 and 8 talk about individual responsibility and introduce the importance of our own personal power channels. Chapter 9 is about amending the Constitution. Chapters 10 and 11 discuss expanding Congress. The last chapters in the book discuss what the Fourth Branch is and why it is critical to our democracy in the twenty-first century and beyond.

The journey is hardly started in one sense; in another sense, this is an outcome of hundreds of years of our history. But we must recognize either way that we are indeed on a journey together, and that we have a say in where the trip will end. Join us in the conversation and the movement to make our democracy healthy in the twenty-first century.

— Guy Terrell and Jack Trammell
Spring 2016

# CHAPTER 1

## Congressional Dysfunction—Time to Fix It

• • •

*We cannot solve our problems with
the same thinking we used when we
created them.*

—Albert Einstein

Every time Congress begins a new session, a world of possibilities opens on the floors of the House of Representatives and the Senate. The lives of current citizens and future generations hang in the balance, as people's representatives have the opportunity to affect change. Too often in these times, by the end of the day or when everyone leaves the chambers for the night, not enough transformational work took place and little progress occurred that can resolve the conflicts between our elected legislators and political parties. Opportunities both great and small fail again and again to see the light of day.

The urgency and desperation of ailing segments of our nation get ignored over and over. Collective problems we all need to see resolved are put off again and again. Voters well understand that disagreement takes place between and within our two primary parties, but our current frustration goes much deeper than that. Conflict and disagreement are often inherent in making laws. But we've moved beyond that, and we, the people, have had enough. We simply have no alternative but to modify our governance.

As voters we can, if we choose, grant ourselves the ability to insert ourselves more directly into the legislative process to change the course of action from one of continual delay to one of continuous forward motion. We have tools available to us that can alleviate the frustration and actually make government move forward and work for us.

Recall the scene from the movie *Patton* where a donkey, stopped

1

on a bridge, held up the advance of a division of the U.S. Third Army. George C. Scott, playing General Patton, pulled out an ivory-handled pistol and shot the animal, threw it into the river, and got back to the important business of carrying on military operations. Although violence is not a suitable option and never part of real change, this anecdote conveys an important truth about our democracy. If we don't react to change and remove obstacles, the collective effort will stall. This imagery mirrors the way voters feel. Congress blocks the progress of the long column of citizen voters who need results and, in most cases, are perfectly willing and able to work toward them and seek solutions.

Therefore, we the people should advance changes to the venerable Constitution to create new methodologies to ensure better governance for our nation. Whatever hardships we face now, more difficult times will arise again and again. There will be donkeys on bridges. We need to update the Constitution to make it fit the twenty-first century and to establish a newer framework for governance that future generations will need when they take the helm. Our system was designed to change when we needed it to, and we are currently in a time to do that.

## Fair Legislation Is an Incredibly Difficult Task

Too many blogs and bloggers comment on the daily activities of the 535 people that make up the Senate and the House of Representatives, and sometimes the noise from this obscures the real challenges. Everyone has something to say about what is done or left undone or what has simply been pushed aside. Congress functions under a microscope with every move reported in myriad media outlets. Because the size of the two bodies is capped at 535, each congressperson represents more and more constituents every year. Legislators become more important simply because they represent a larger number of constituents.

The membership of the House of Representatives was capped at 435 members in 1929. The population of the country at that time was 121 million people. Congress is a pipe trying to transport more than it was designed to carry. Being a member of Congress is by definition a tough and frustrating job. We the people can help make changes to solve not just the problem of congressional dysfunction but actually make it easier for our representatives to do their jobs.

Currently, political parties have one goal, it seems—to make the other one look incompetent. (At least they agree on that.) As a result, the party in the minority seeks to slow the agenda of the majority party as much as possible. Each party focuses on blocking the other side's agenda. To use an analogy from World War I, both parties have dug trenches and created a no-compromise area between them with mines and barbed wire. As a result, America as a nation is not going anywhere.

One prime example of the standstill we are experiencing can be seen in the history of constitutional amendments. Our founders intended that the Constitution be a living document and anticipated that it would need changes and updates. Until recent times, amendments were a difficult but necessary national dialogue about our democracy. Once more, we advocate reform of our legislative framework with constitutional amendments to alter the course and outcome of the future and to end the standstill in Washington, D.C.

This task that is the subject of this book—growing a Fourth Branch of government—is a sacred duty. We can no longer ignore the necessity for change, even as we are mindful of the hard-won rights and freedoms already embedded in the current U.S. Constitution and its amendments. We must act the way a surgeon approaches a patient and first do no harm. But, like a patient who cannot digest all of her food and suffers from indigestion, we know there is a blockage that must be addressed.

## Congressional Duties

Congress has a wide-ranging job description as laid out in the Constitution. The Constitution exists to keep the United States running smoothly and also, due to our stature, guides us in our duties to the rest of the world. Section 8 enumerates congressional obligations:

*The Congress shall have Power To lay and collect Taxes, Duties, Imposts and Excises, to pay the Debts and provide for the common Defence and general Welfare of the United States; but all Duties, Imposts and Excises shall be uniform throughout the United States;*
1. *To borrow Money on the credit of the United States;*
2. *To regulate Commerce with foreign Nations, and among the several States, and with the Indian Tribes;*

3. *To establish an uniform Rule of Naturalization, and uniform Laws on the subject of Bankruptcies throughout the United States;*

4. *To coin Money, regulate the Value thereof, and of foreign Coin, and fix the Standard of Weights and Measures;*

5. *To provide for the Punishment of counterfeiting the Securities and current Coin of the United States;*

6. *To establish Post Offices and post Roads;*

7. *To promote the Progress of Science and useful Arts, by securing for limited Times to Authors and Inventors the exclusive Right to their respective Writings and Discoveries;*

8. *To constitute Tribunals inferior to the supreme Court;*

9. *To define and punish Piracies and Felonies committed on the high Seas, and Offences against the Law of Nations;*

10. *To declare War, grant Letters of Marque and Reprisal, and make Rules concerning Captures on Land and Water;*

11. *To raise and support Armies, but no Appropriation of Money to that Use shall be for a longer Term than two Years;*

12. *To provide and maintain a Navy;*

13. *To make Rules for the Government and Regulation of the land and naval Forces;*

14. *To provide for calling forth the Militia to execute the Laws of the Union, suppress Insurrections and repel Invasions;*

15. *To provide for organizing, arming, and disciplining, the Militia, and for governing such Part of them as may be employed in the Service of the United States, reserving to the States respectively, the Appointment of the Officers, and the Authority of training the Militia according to the discipline prescribed by Congress;*

16. *To exercise exclusive Legislation in all Cases whatsoever, over such District (not exceeding ten Miles square) as may, by Cession of particular States, and the Acceptance of Congress, become the Seat of the Government of the United States, and to exercise like Authority over all Places purchased by the Consent of the Legislature of the State in which the Same shall be, for the Erection of Forts, Magazines, Arsenals, dock-Yards, and other needful Buildings;—And*

17. *To make all Laws which shall be necessary and proper for carrying into Execution the foregoing Powers, and all other Powers vested by this Constitution in the Government of the United States, or in any Department or Officer thereof.*

In short, Congress must keep the machinery of government working properly at all times and, we might add, across all generations. With that much at stake, to block bills that would actually address some of those responsibilities would seem an outright neglect of critical job duties. Shutting down the government makes it more difficult for it to fulfill its duties, let alone consider more effective ways to fulfill those duties.

The Fourth Branch should hold our elected officials responsible. By the end of this book, the role of the Fourth Branch and its right to step in whenever these duties are not fulfilled will become increasingly clear. There should be other duties added to the above list of congressional duties to reflect additional responsibilities that have arisen over the last two hundred years. It's time for an update.

## The Long Crescendo of Congressional Dysfunction

The causes for dysfunction fill many books, magazines, websites, and news clips already. Studies by the Pew Research Center show that the population tends to align with one party or the other and then to vote along party lines without much variation. When voters tend to cast their ballots strictly along hard party lines, the results of elections increasingly show up in partisan Congresses.

Jonathan Haidt of New York University says that, historically, Congress has been very polarized. He argues that the mid-twentieth century was an anomaly and we should expect this polarization as the norm. Coming out of World War II, Congress felt a greater sense of shared purpose as a result of the defeat of a common enemy. Haidt presents a detailed analysis of the causes and some possible solutions at a website that is aimed at improving civility and our ability to disagree productively (http://www.civilpolitics.org/content/the-ten-causes-of-americas-political-dysfunction/). Nevertheless, voters remain angry that Congress can't seem to get anything accomplished, and there is evidence that we are becoming more partisan rather than less. We continue to vote along party lines even though most people think of themselves as Independents not beholden to one party or the other. (We are dysfunctional as voters.) When we decide on a candidate, we tend to vote for others from that party's roster even if we do not always feel we belong to one party or the other.

5

Assuming Haidt to be correct that the normal functioning of Congress leads to polarization and resistance to another party's changes, we should seek democratic solutions to gridlock and partisanship and re-conceptualize how our representatives work. We can accept the current situation as fact and then figure out what to do about it. We must establish new techniques for resolving conflicts and disagreements. Failure to address this doesn't just destroy the other party's agenda but, in the long run, destroys our citizens and our future and our ability to work together.

Of course, voters often disagree on what should be done. That is why we vote to begin with. But once in Washington, D.C., our representatives have to work for everyone, and not just for one party. Some members of Congress have occasionally had enough of the current impasse and simply resigned in frustration. Instead of an opportunity for change, voters often respond to such resignations by electing even more partisan candidates. Like a family that is dysfunctional, it tends to get worse year by year.

Consider the decline of productivity of Congress in the graph below:

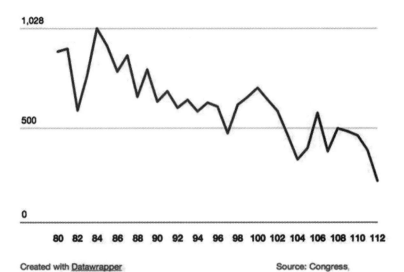

Created with Datawrapper                                           Source: Congress,
http://cf.datawrapper.de/962eHV2/ Sat Apr 05 2014 15:59:39 GMT-0400 (EDT)

The lower scale is the congressional session starting with the eightieth, which met from January 3, 1947 to January 3, 1949. The totals are for the two-year session. The graph is an oversimplification because some laws are more complex than others. To get a more detailed rating, each law would have to be assigned a rating number and then recompiled. However, the general trend and direction is valid, and of concern.

An independent voter, stuck with only two political parties who put forth candidates, inevitably becomes frustrated with some of the narrow choices available. This brings us back to the data that suggests that many Americans identify with being independent, even if they ultimately are forced to shelter in one party or the other. Democracy fails when vast numbers of voters would actually choose something or someone else if available, yet the system prevents it.

By the time a candidate has made it through fundraising and primaries, he or she has become firmly locked into a committed, often partisan agenda. Today, more and more constituents identify themselves as independent as they cannot identify with the total agenda of one party or the other. Voters, even in heavily Republican or Democratic districts, have more variation across individual issues than can be summed up in one candidate or another. Voters can only select Candidate A or B with a belief system set by the party they represent. Each voter generally has some conservative views and some liberal views. The ballot is not a cafeteria menu where we can pick and choose positions to support. We have to select the best overall position and hold our nose.

In 1995, the Republican Party gained the majority in the House of Representatives. For forty years, 1955 to 1995, the Democratic Party held the majority (although ideologically there was a lot of division). The Republican Party in 1995 formed a new strategy to win elections. Newt Gingrich formed the Conservative Opportunity Society to expand Republican ideas. As a result, the Republican Party controlled the speakership again. Although the realignment of strategies focused on gaining or retaining power, the Republican Revolution also unwittingly showed two other things: first, that a populist movement could influence the direction of politics, and second, that a revolution confined to the current three branches was doomed to fall into an old pattern. The next revolution must include the Fourth Branch.

By the time Democrats regained the majority for four years starting in 2007, they did not bring back the days of letting the minority party offer alternative bills. In fact, the House minority now plays a vastly diminished role, and both parties spend huge effort trying to gain or hold the majority. The potential fruit of the Republican Revolution was lost to both parties.

Like the Montagues and Capulets, our parties are locked in permanent disagreement, which can have unpredictable and very unpleasant results. We all bear responsibility for this situation, since congressional dysfunction is the logical result of closed primaries, too many gerrymandered one-party seats, and low-turnout elections. These factors are not governed by constitutional law, but by choices people can make at the state level. Government shutdowns, filibusters, and blocked appointments are the tools Congresspersons now use. These tactics short-circuit every process and precedence for proper discussion and legislation. As Shakespeare would say, "All are punishéd."

In a comment on this situation, William J. Bennett said, "We are in the midst of a serious philosophical battle over the future of this country—a battle between a small, limited government system and a big government entitlement state. The nature of our Constitution requires that the American people decide the direction of this country, not Washington. And until the American people decide, there will be arguments, division and gridlock." Bennett quotes James Madison from the "Federalist No. 10," suggesting human nature and normal discourse make up the fabric of disagreements. But we will need to find a way to replace the dysfunction with methods for effective resolution of disagreements. In other words, to disagree is normal; to do nothing as a result is not normal

We will propose changes to the Constitution that will establish a different framework to enable a larger national discussion as we face our biggest problems. The Fourth Branch is a way to widen the pipe to handle the load.

Voters deplore the way Congress acts. The opinion we have of our elected officials is one of the lowest ever. But we are also ambivalent about deciding whether the time has come to do something about it. When, not if, we decide we must alter the Constitution, we will have an inherent fear that we might make it worse instead of better. When we decide we need to update the kitchen or bathroom in our home, we hesitate because of the disruption that comes with it. If you wait too long, the old appliances all fail and the floors rot out. We must face the reality that if we ignore the current stalemate, nothing will change, and, in fact, our democracy will deteriorate.

Stein Ringen, a British scholar, wrote a series of Internet articles published in October 2014 for opendemocracy.net, a not-for-profit digital commons that seeks out and debates forms of democratic change. The series editor comments that American democracy (from the perspective of the British Isles) has always been "messy, rough and unruly" but has always come through. "Even so, democracy has delivered and made America not only the world's supreme power but also its lighthouse socially and culturally." We quote these statements because it places the dysfunction we see in a larger context. People look to America for leadership in the evolution of democracy. That is a promise we can only fulfill when we act bravely, and are honest with ourselves about the reality we face.

Mr. Ringen states that Congress is not doing its job because it's not providing the governing America requires. His surprising contention is that Congress has lost power to the other branches and that dysfunction results from that loss.

> *Not only does Congress not check the other powers, it does not do its part of the joint job of governing. The budget is out of control with huge deficits. Congress complains but does not create order. The tax system is a nightmare that combines all the vices that are possible in taxation – inefficient in raising revenues, unfair, offensive to taxpayers and in the burdens of compliance it heaps on them, and distorting and discouraging to business – and Congress stands by and lets the chaos deepen. The tax code grew from 1.4 million words in 2001 to 3.8 million in 2010, in a continuous introduction of new loopholes. Social security [sic] is in financial disarray, but while most European governments have overhauled their systems to make them sustainable, American politicians are stuck in a fruitless debate for or against reform. The country's infrastructure in transport and communications*

*is poor and eroding, and Congress lets it slide. There is a desperate need for control in issues such as immigration and gun use, but Congress leaves disorder to prevail. Obstructive members of Congress blame others, of course, the president in particular, but the failing institution in America's constitutional system is Congress itself.*

The current situation has as many causes as commentators can come up with. Arguing about the definitive cause will waste energy and provide very little additional insight. Our journey into a Fourth Branch will establish another political revolution, not only resolving the current situation but showing us a template for how we continue to reinvent our democracy. No reverse road exists, but we do have forks in the road in front of us. Congress will not be able to undo its dysfunction without the help of the Fourth Branch. The voters of this country must provide the solution as is both our right and our duty as defined in the Constitution. We are not sheep that need to be herded from one field to another. We are responsible for building new gateways to new ideas.

The thirteen original states between 1781 and 1789 did not make up a nation. A rag-tag set of state legislatures battled for the well-being of its inhabitants after British rule ended and there were no more royal governors. States had to write their own constitutions. Governance had to be created anew. The key leaders of those times created the structure, framework, and commerce of a nation. States became part of a national framework only with the implementation of the Constitution. We, as a nation, are a miracle. We must roll up our sleeves again and come together to figure out how to improve our democracy for this century and beyond.

Congress will continue its work, but alongside them we will build the new framework. These are difficult times, but we may face even more difficult times. Our nation can face them through a healthier democracy.

# CHAPTER 2

## The Challenge for Democracy in the Twenty-first Century and Beyond

• • •

*Though no one can go back and make a brand new start, anyone can start from now and make a brand new ending.*

—Carl Bard

We own a long, long tradition of collective success and expanded rights and opportunity. But that tradition is under stress. We are like an undefeated team having a bad quarter. We need to huddle and plan a strategy to turn the game back in our direction. It is obvious that our current game plan and play execution is flawed. In fact, our founders intended that we be able to embrace changes we need. Alexis de Tocqueville said in *Democracy in America*, published in 1835, that a danger for America is that we might become too fearful of change.

> *I cannot help fearing that men may reach a point where they look on every new theory as a danger, every innovation as a toilsome trouble, every social advance as a first step toward revolution, and that they may absolutely refuse to move at all for fear of being carried off their feet. The prospect really does frighten me that they may finally become so engrossed in a cowardly love of immediate pleasures that their interest in their own future and in that of their descendants may vanish, and that they will prefer tamely to follow the course of their destiny rather than make a sudden energetic effort necessary to set things right.*

We must always be aggressive in examining our position on the field and remain focused on the long-term goals that will benefit everyone. De Tocqueville had the advantage of viewing America from an outside perspective. For us to see where we really are, we must be honest about who our players are and where we are in the game. That will mean setting goals for our nation collectively with both parties pushing in the same direction.

In this game, Republicans and Democrats ultimately play on the same team. We cannot be the Democratic Party on one team and the Republican Party on the other team even though there are real differences in party platforms. We can, however, find the common ground and move forward from there. The primary purpose of the Fourth Branch is not to set specific agenda items but to set in motion an examination of the present and future ways we will govern ourselves.

As citizens of the United States, we can no longer ignore our collective responsibility to recognize, assess, and create solutions for the challenges our nation faces. We can name a few of them without having to look very far, the nature of immigration, the expansion of voting rights, or how we limit the influence of money in politics and campaigning. Solutions can differ, but what can't be compromised is creating a framework where solutions can actually be realized.

Like water rising behind a dam, our government faces increasing numbers of complex challenges every year, and this rain will neither cease nor let up. We can no longer cast our ballots and then callously return to our own pursuits, leaving all decisions to elected officials, while the ruling parties engage in partisan politics that prevent viable solutions to all the problems that threaten to overwhelm us.

The framework that will allow solutions is one that is consistent with who we are in the twenty-first century. We are an Internet-driven culture where everything happens fast. We are part of a global economy. We have a democracy driven by big money. Any solution like the Fourth Branch will have to create a framework consistent with who and where we are.

This book proposes one or more National Constitutional Conventions to hammer out a new framework. Such a framework will enable our nation to update our democracy and put in place changes in the Constitution of our republic that will make our governance more effective and efficient. This goal is not unrealistic. It is consistent with our vision, our abilities, and is within our grasp. It is in harmony with the intent of our Founding Fathers.

If we fail to act, our governance will become increasingly reactionary. We will no longer be in control of our own destiny. We cannot ignore this situation for much longer without putting future generations at risk.

Every day our nation writes the story of its life and our new history. Some chapters tell of triumphs the way a novel about high school shows how a young woman overcame some early childhood disease or growing up in a poor neighborhood yet goes on to shoot the winning shot in a basketball game or to break the serve of another player in a tennis tournament and win the set. Other chapters reveal the obstacles to dreams, loss, and sometimes untimely death. Our history is not always on a continual upward slope. What happens to each of us, good and bad, creates the inks that make up the print of our nation's history.

We must continually step up to make the story ending what we want it to be. An eight-year-old girl from Richmond, Virginia, Alyvia Hathaway, raised money to provide help for the homeless in Richmond's Monroe Park and recruited others to participate in the Central Virginia Kidney Walk in October 2014. She said her grandmother told her, "If you don't like what you see, change it."

The Founding Fathers expressed the same sentiment. "Give me liberty, or give me death."

Commentators, journalists, and politicians from across the political spectrum say more and more frequently that our system is breaking or already broken. Mann and Ornstein referred to Congress as the broken branch in their book, *The Broken Branch: How Congress Is Failing America and How to Get It Back on Track*. Too often as citizens, we feel powerless to change this situation. Many voters express their hopelessness by simply throwing up their hands and refusing to go to the polls. As voters, we feel like our Congress is a manager that makes decisions that do not seem to foster the best interests of the company we both work for. In a case like that, most people will look for another job under a different manager either within or outside of the company.

We cannot abandon our country. Each year, the situation under a bad manager gets more toxic. But we cannot fire Congress and we've had poor luck electing replacements that can resolve the situation or act differently. It's time for new approaches. It's time for a Fourth Branch.

*There is in America today pervasive concern about the basic functioning of our democracy. Congress is viewed less favorably than ever before in the history of public opinion polling. Revulsion at political figures unable to reach agreement on measures that substantially reduce prospective budget deficits is widespread. Pundits and politicians alike condemn gridlock as angry movements like Occupy Wall Street and the Tea Party emerge on both sides of the political spectrum, and partisanship seems to become ever more pervasive.*

*All this comes at a time of great challenge. Profound changes, as emerging economies led by China converge toward the West, will redefine the global order. Beyond the current economic downturn, which is surely the most serious since the Great Depression, lies the even more serious challenge of the rise of technologies that may well raise average productivity but displace large numbers of workers. Public debt is running up in a way that is without precedent except in times of all-out war. And a combination of the share of the population that is aged and the rising relative price of public services such as healthcare and education pressures future budgets.*

*Anyone who has worked in a political position in Washington has had ample experience with great frustration. Almost everyone involved with public policy feels as I do that there is much that is essential yet infeasible in the current political environment. Yet context is important. Concerns about gridlock are a near-constant in American political history and in important respects reflect desirable checks and balances; much more progress is occurring in key sectors than is usually acknowledged; and American decision making, for all its flaws, stands up well in global comparison.*

—Lawrence Summers, April 15, 2013

*We know our political system is broken. The signs are everywhere: knee-jerk partisanship, massive debts and unfunded liabilities, widespread citizen dissatisfaction, trillion-dollar deficits, rampant public and private corruption, and a federal government that has less support than King George III at the time of the American Revolution.*

*But fixing the system is a staggeringly complex undertaking. The causes of its dysfunction are deep and obscure.*

—Leo Linbeck, III, *The American Conservative*

## America Is in Long-term Jeopardy Because of a Lack of Congressional Decisions

Our democracy, as even school children know, consists of three branches. In spite of the founders' wisdom in creating checks and balances, all three branches are not equal. The legislative branch has arguably become the most powerful and yet has also become the branch must vulnerable to the current weaknesses in our system. There are 535 members of Congress, and when they collectively go up for reelection, billions of dollars flood the landscape and influence the outcome. In contrast, Supreme Court justices are appointed for life, with in theory no money involved.

Congress is where change can and should occur.

Throughout history, many warnings have gone unheeded. Warnings cannot all be verified, or perhaps the source is deemed unreliable. Warnings of icebergs near the Titanic did not deter the White Star Line from their quest to set an Atlantic crossing record. Churchill warned the world repeatedly to heed the threat of Nazi Germany in 1938 and 1939. An operator, Jimmy Harrell, on the Deepwater Horizon oil rig warned a British Petroleum official that they should use "heavy mud," a more expensive product to control the gas coming out of the drilling. In 1985, a year before the space shuttle Challenger disaster, an engineer, Roger Boisjoly with Morton Thiokol, warned that joints sealing sections of a solid rocket booster could fail if they got too cold.

On a personal level, we warn young people not to drive too fast or to text while driving, to pay attention to other drivers on the road, to avoid drugs. We tell our friends to avoid certain kinds of investments, to watch what they eat, to stay out of debt. Most advice and warnings go unheeded. The world and most of us survive anyway and to heed every warning would slow down progress, pleasure, or profit (take your pick). History holds thousands of examples of heeded and unheeded warnings that changed outcomes. An Indian scout, Mitch Bouyer (his Anglicized name), warned Custer of the large size of Sitting Bull's camp, and that there were many warriors encamped there. We all know the ending of that story.

America is filled with warning signs about the failing health of democracy today. The founders created a legislative process in the Constitution that allows us as a people to address the problems. The question is whether we are willing and ready to do so. Budget sequestration, low voter turnout, overt gerrymandering—all of the signs are there if we are willing to see them.

We have no time to lose. We must approach this challenge the way Luke Skywalker did when Yoda said to him, "Do. Or do not. There is no try." Your nation has arrived at an important juncture. We put the resources of our nation to work after World War II with the Marshall Plan to help Europe. We stopped the invasion of South Korea in the Korean War. We helped bring down the Iron Curtain. We have sent aid to dozens of countries over decades. We have recently sent our troops into Iraq and Afghanistan.

We need to spend our money, time, and talent on ourselves this time. We have tried to help other nations establish democratic constitutions. Let's examine what we need to change in our Constitution to make it better. Would the example we offer today encourage an emerging democracy to adopt our present Constitution? If the answer is no, we need to reshape our nation to put us back at the front of the democracy parade.

A primary goal should be to reconsider the work of Congress as a body that can create more effective laws and spend less time in gridlock. Although more does not always equal better, in this case there is growing historical data to show that Congress is accomplishing less and less each session it meets.

Rather than list all of the issues here, we suggest that you turn on a news program tonight. You will likely hear about some member of Congress who has acted unethically, a story about partisan gridlock in a state or national legislative body or else about the danger of war somewhere. What you are not likely to hear is that a bipartisan bill that helps some group of people or solves a pervasive problem has been passed and is now being signed by the president.

Do you feel that you could easily call up your congressional representative and have a conversation with them about this?

Most of us would answer this in the negative, or even think, why bother?

Americans must not despair. We have tools in our Constitutional tool shed that can be used in this setting. Our duty is to state as clearly and calmly as possible that the way our government works at present cannot be sustained indefinitely; dysfunction cannot be argued or wished away. When our grandfathers passed away, they left us their old tools in the barn where they stored hay. The wooden handles of the tools they left us were split or worn out. To use those tools again, we had to replace most of the handles.

Our Constitution represents the shed where we store the tools of government. Some of those tools need new handles. In this book, we urge all voters to take action to set a new course for our republic, a course that will implement a wider participation on a continual basis by voters. If enough voters finally demand specific changes, we will see action. In fact, new tools can go into the shed that our forefathers could not even imagine!

Current members of Congress may not be ready to see the system change. Voters have the power, however, to demand a Fourth Branch. We can always hope that our extreme partisanship and the decline of the middle class is a temporary phenomenon, and it will right itself soon enough. But what harm could come if we improve our governance by changing the Constitution to make governing more effective before we are assured that we must make needed repairs? Do we wait until the middle class has ceased to exist? Do we just keep building more prisons? Aren't they full enough now? Too often, our Congress treats symptoms rather than causes.

Maybe yet another commission could be appointed to study how to update the republic. That would be an excellent way to blunt the momentum that builds year by year for changes to Congress and kill any chance at real change. Instead, the voters hold the power to be the ultimate commission. The sacred beliefs in the structures established in the Constitution are the only way to govern our nation and prevent the weakening that has continued year after year. It's time for an update to the software.

The idea for a Fourth Branch suggests a very simple concept—a branch of government designed to allow citizen voters a more direct say in the way we are governed. And when Congress fails to act, then the people may do so.

Large swaths of our cities and population live in what most of us would call substandard conditions. We think that only those we elect to Congress have the power and responsibility to take care of this, but many great civilizations have failed when they become self-satisfied. Citizens hand over their power to others, pursue life's pleasures, and ignore those less fortunate. We have two distinct duties. One, to modify the workings of our republic so that compromise and bipartisanship can flourish at all times, and, two, to establish new institutions that will lift up all members of society while setting an example to other nations of the evolution of democracy. No one gets a free ride. Debts are not paper money only. There is a debt we owe to our own souls and to the soul of our nation.


## We Think Congress, Not Ourselves, Must Take Action

We might expect Congress to come up with conflict-resolution methodologies after so many years of severe partisanship that prevented compromise on issues so that needed prompt attention. Much needed laws, spending bills, and various appointments languished in committee or simply were never put to a vote. No party can expect to be in control of Congress continuously. Even children in school are taught to get along with those who are different. But evidence suggests that when one party cannot get its way in American politics, it throws up roadblocks whenever it can.

From October 1 through October 16, 2013, the United States federal government shut down and curtailed most routine operations because neither legislation appropriating funds for fiscal year 2014 nor a continuing resolution for the interim authorization of appropriations for fiscal year 2014 was enacted in time. Regular government operations resumed October 17 after an interim appropriations bill was signed into law. We've endured eighteen government shutdowns since 1976 under both Democratic and Republican Congresses. Cumulatively, these amounted to 128 days when we paid for services we did not get since most workers got paid for time on furlough. Approximately one third of those days took place in the last twenty years under first Bill Clinton and then Barack Obama.

The impression most voters have is that things are getting worse. Congress should not be able to shut down our government simply because they can't reach consensus. Allowing them to do nothing and at the same time crippling our nation as a result is a not a sterling example of democracy in action. Shutdown is not a tactic so much as a bludgeon. If the United States were to be actually bankrupted, then such an action might make sense. But we're not bankrupt, and we deserve better. Congress shows its declining effectiveness in those situations.

Why hasn't Congress come up with new amendments? If we live in a house where the roof leaks, we set out buckets to catch the water. We might call those continuing resolutions. But if the roof keeps leaking year after year, wouldn't we plan to repair the roof? Friends, it's time to call a roofer—a National Constitutional Convention.

You'll recall from Chapter 1 the graph that demonstrated the decline of productivity of numerous congressional sessions. The number of bills passed by Congress during two-year sessions between 1974 and 2014 dramatically went down.

The pace of congressional activity is unlikely to accelerate much from here in the next twenty years if nothing changes. How low could this graph go, we wonder? What would that mean? Perhaps the complexity of our problems makes it difficult to write new legislation. Perhaps after solving all the really big problems, Congress only has left those problems that require more nuanced solutions and are genuinely harder to solve.

Or, could it be that the world has grown more complicated, and, at the same time, Congress has become less effective?

Juxtapose the decline in congressional productivity during roughly this same period with the compensation of employees as a portion of the Gross Domestic Product, which also shows a similar decline. This chart, from the St. Louis Federal Reserve, covers a longer period of time. But focus on the period where both the graph on page

6 and this one overlap.

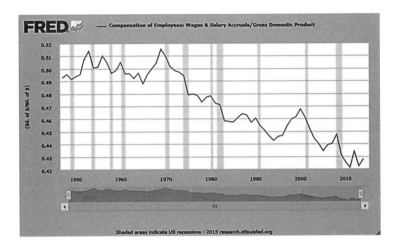

From about 1980 to 2014, the number of bills passed by Congress declined by approximately 63½ percent. During that same time frame, total wages as a percentage of GDP declined by a little over 11 percent. We cannot unequivocally state that the declines shown in these two graphs are in any way related, but our curiosity is raised. And notice the rise in productivity of Congress and the increase in compensation during the Clinton years in the White House.

From 1976, the GDP of all goods and services sold in the United States went from $2 trillion to $16.7 trillion in 2013, according to the World Bank. Our overall compensation went from about 48 percent of GDP or $960 billion in 1976 to 42 percent of GDP or $7 trillion in 2013. So while GDP rose 835 percent during that time, wages rose by 725 percent. If wages as percent of GDP had remained steady in 2013, total compensation would have been about $1 trillion more in the last year reported. And had wages as a percentage of GDP remained steady, it would have been more in each year. It's not just wages that are going down for most of the working population, but overall wealth is going down as well. The working classes would also have been paying more taxes on the money we might have made. Maybe our deficit would be less as well. You don't need to be an economist to interpret these numbers. Even without these charts, other indicators from economists prove that most people are getting poorer.

Another example is one that hits home for many parents of

college-age students, who after they graduate must still live at home and make less than their parents made in actual dollars when they graduated twenty years earlier. What are the odds these college grads will be better off than their parents and grandparents? Does Congress have any responsibility for this situation?

We are stockholders in the United States of America. We want a better return on our inputs and efforts. When managers don't produce the results stockholders expect, the boards of directors of companies often bring in a new team. When a board of directors does not take action to fix an ailing company, outsiders might buy up shares and get elected to those boards to make change happen. This book is about beginning a similar kind of makeover of the way we run our company, our United States. We can transform our republic using the power to amend the Constitution.

## The Wrong Response—Find a Root Cause or at Least Place Blame

It is human nature to want to uncover the cause of a problem. When the root of a problem can be pinpointed, a solution can be designed and put in place. We choose to blame Congress, lobbyists, and political parties for our current problems, thinking that some obstreperous individuals must be identified. If there is a problem, there must also be a fundamental cause—some cause at the heart of congressional dysfunction. We operate inside a detective or forensic framework, always looking for someone to blame or the cause when something goes wrong. Why is there a growing gap between the rich and the poor? What was the cause of the financial collapse in 2008? Who is to blame when a costly military weapon does not live up to its promise? Why can't we get funds for infrastructure projects? Why are our schools so bad?

Too much focus on blame can either prevent or delay reasonable solutions. The blame game ends here. It has gone on long enough. It may sound as if we blame Congress for many ills. Instead, we say that continuing to drive an old car (the original, out-of-date Constitution) will result in the need for constant repairs no matter who is driving. A change in voter and congressional behavior could end the stalemate we have been discussing, but we also need a framework to allow voters a better opportunity to interact with the legislative process and to vote more easily regardless of how Congress gets along.

We have laws that need to be passed and also laws requiring repeal and revision. We have laws made by those who could not have anticipated all the variables that came into play after some laws went into effect. Writing laws is difficult work and not to be taken lightly. We don't give enough praise for the good that Congress does. In extreme cases, the courts have become involved. The courts are the last resort, and they either define how the law will be interpreted and applied or they must overturn it. In the case of overturned laws, Congress will have to revisit the law and revise it.

Congress is far from perfect. In fairness, the Constitution has never been perfect either. Our founders chose not to deal with the status of slaves and women as citizen voters. The founders designed a system that fit their times and that has worked very well for most of our history. But now we are running up against some of the gaps in the Constitution when applying an eighteenth-century framework to twenty-first-century-and-beyond problems, problems that Madison and others could not foresee.

We have an outdated vehicle, and Congress needs our help to deal with some of the issues that define our time. Our system of legislation leaves too many people underrepresented. It cannot respond quickly enough to some changes (which can be a good thing in some cases). But the Constitution and congressional rules can too easily be manipulated to delay change. Those rules need to be updated more now than ever before. Individuals alone didn't create our current dysfunction. We cannot say that if we had better men and women in Congress then all of our partisanship would vanish. The way the system works must be modified to manage the friction that exists naturally among individuals, parties, and systems but doesn't also bring legislation to standstill and prevent national progress.

## We Mutually Pledge to Each Other Our Lives, Our Fortunes, and Our Sacred Honor

Before we enter into a list of suggestions for changes to the Constitution, we must remind ourselves of the concluding words from the Declaration of Independence. We must begin with a firm belief in mutual benefits to be achieved by any changes. When the signers of the Declaration of Independence chose to stand up for independence, they risked everything. They were going up against a world power that had just won a number of wars and whose navy and army were considered the best at that time.

What we will propose in what follows represents more than the mechanics of government and changes in its operations. We must include not only a pledge not to harm anyone, but also the belief that our hopes and dreams ride alongside our quest for new efficiency and effectiveness. If voters conclude that the Constitution needs to be changed, we need to approach it with a sense of sacred duty, the same way the founders did. Too much is at stake for future generations.

A key concept will be a willingness to think with newness. We must un-vilify each other. We must speak for others as well as ourselves. We must believe in an enlarged future for everyone. We must discover new solutions and new options. We must embrace a new set of ideals, invent them when necessary. We must be ambitious for our nation and each other. We must envision an enlarged republic built on the one we already have.

In addition to a willingness to think in new ways, we will need to exhibit courage, determination, and compromise to make changes to our governance. Our nation is more globally impacted than ever before. We had been able to isolate ourselves from many dangers until the twentieth century. We are now impacted more than ever by global events to a degree that makes governing more difficult.

We need to be open to unexpected opportunities. Perhaps like the U.S. Olympic team beating Russia in ice hockey in 1980 at Lake Placid, we will experience a miracle in Washington. (And perhaps the Fourth Branch will result in something new *outside* of Washington.) It's not beyond the human imagination that the president, Congress, and the Supreme Court could assemble jointly and redesign their own workings to reset the course of the United States to deal with the present challenges and those of future generations. But until they do so, we had better make our own plans.

What brings about the advance of truly great nations? Churchill said it is "a cause which rouses the spontaneous surgings of the human spirit in millions of hearts—these have proved to be the decisive factors in the human story." We, as citizens of the United States of America, are compelled to preserve the core principles that have provided such great benefits for so many going forward. By doing so, we will increase the bounty and richness of our nation for everyone, including those who have until now only known impotence or poverty of thought and action. Nothing has to remain the way it is indefinitely.

## High-Level Roadmap

The Constitution is designed to enable changes that will help us build the framework to solve future problems. The creation of the Fourth Branch is such a framework for the present times. Our goal is lifting the well-being of our citizens through lawmaking with more dynamic input from voters. This will necessarily mean plowing new ground, suggesting different solutions, and laying out new amendments that will become part of the Constitution, a living framework for problems that are not even defined yet.

The unique problems that we face in the United States are compounded by low voter turnout. Part of the reason for that low turnout is that many voters feel disenfranchised by the system, a system that can be characterized by elections swayed by big money, career politicians who become powerful but sometimes ineffective incumbents, and gridlock in Congress that essentially signals voters that their voice rarely comes through.

It is natural that people generally won't want major changes to the republic unless they perceive an even greater benefit. People who do not currently vote may not feel qualified enough to have a say in the future of the Constitution or may not even understand the historical importance of updating the Constitution. It was that way when the Republic formed—many founders returned home from national meetings to convince their constituents of the need for change. But if, on the remote possibility, a majority in our modern democracy wanted to change the shape of our republic, here's what would have to take place.

We would need to launch a movement similar to the Civil Rights Movement that would join all the organizations that want basic changes, from the League of Women Voters to the American Conservative Union. We would have to define clear strategic goals and objectives, and then act in a united way.

The foundation of the change will be the requirement to unfragment the beliefs and ideas that we each of us individually hold that keep us separated from unified action. Our entrenched political parties are so set in their divisive patterns that we can't imagine someone leaving one to join the other, and yet all of us have beliefs that span broader spectrums than a single party. We need to make it safe to belong to groups without it being an all-or-nothing proposition.

This kind of endeavor will demand that we interact without the normal barriers and defenses we use to protect ourselves. We need to think and act as one. When our nation made great progress or stood together in the past, it came from a sense of working for a common purpose, usually with an external threat to our well-being. That threat is not Congress or the Constitution—they are the symptoms. The underlying cause is our reluctance to change the way we govern in the twenty-first century. That threat is a future with challenges for everyone, with problems for everyone, with potential financial icebergs, but the biggest danger is our restricted lack of ability to respond.

## The Changes We Propose

We envision three basic constitutional changes that would still need additional layers of laws to detail the way they would be implemented. We will cover these in the chapters that follow. But here is the high-level view.

One, establish a more flexible voting mechanism. Allow electronic voting when an election takes place and establish a voting window of several days so that anyone who has the right to vote can do so with minimal difficulty. In short, do away with a single voting day on the Tuesday following the first Monday in November. It needs to be four days to a week long during the last quarter of the year.

Two, enlarge Congress to make it more representative. Every year as our population grows, Congress becomes less representative— never a goal of the founders. Enlarge the House of Representatives to twelve hundred and let representatives live in their own homes in their own districts. They would have an office in town, meet through video conferencing, and meet in plenary session like a convention in different cities across the country as needed, three to four times a year. The Senate could be expanded to 130 by adding thirty at-large senators to represent large parts of the population that are underrepresented in that chamber.

Three, establish a Fourth Branch where any qualified voter could participate in the governance of his/her nation. The rights and responsibilities of the Fourth Branch would need to be debated and defined before they can be laid out. However, generally speaking, it would be a voter-based forum with the ability to interact with the other three branches. It would be a conduit through which some laws could be created that go directly to the president. It could also propose actionable items to Congress to consider. It could handle items that Congress is unable to address for whatever reason (for example, like raising the minimum wage). Here is a very rough timeframe for how long it might take to make changes of this magnitude.

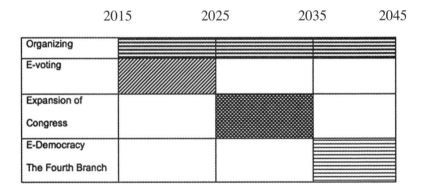

## How to Get There

To make changes of this breadth and magnitude will require both vision and hard grassroots work. The Civil Rights Movement of the sixties had its televised moments but it consisted of a lot more door-to-door organizing and education up and down the back roads. In fact, much of the Civil Rights Movement occurred in less-heralded ways in the decades prior to the sixties. Citizens of our nation may want to complain about Congress, but to develop the interest in doing something about it is quite another thing altogether. Years of education, debate, and persuasion will be required. Nothing of value can be easily created. But we can set our sights on achieving the steps along the way.

We will need to define our common causes and work towards them and let discouragement be only a temporary state. Churchill said, "Never, never, in nothing great or small, large or petty, never give in except to convictions of honour and good sense. Never yield to force; never yield to the apparently overwhelming might of the [other side]." The spur that will keep us headed in the right direction will be the nightly news. Unless Congress and our two political parties suddenly reform and act differently, we will continually be reminded to keep at the task. That's what the founders intended—an iterative, interactive, adapting democracy.

## First Step—Update How We Vote

When our first Congress met, we carried exports in the holds of wooden sailing vessels and trundled farm produce to town on Election Day in carts pulled by horses. We plowed our fields with oxen. Representatives and senators held the first sessions of Congress in Federal Hall in New York City, where they met face-to-face, just as they do now.

We have increasingly sophisticated tools available to us in commerce and communication. We can track people and products like we never could before. We could modernize our democracy to the same extent we have our commerce. With all of the technological and efficiency-oriented advances in communications, why do we continue to vote and enact laws the same way they did then? We will propose e-voting at all levels as the first step—national first, state second. Additionally, we need to take the view that improvements we make will not only enhance our times, but future generations as well. This could become the re-founding of the American republic that was intended.

Our nation in the twenty-first century operates electronically and with more efficiency and effectiveness because of tools that even school children use. Our democracy must be updated to enable better governance, and embrace the times and resources we have at our disposal. To make the changes that follow, we will have to have a great national discussion—a discussion carried out in schools, in electronic town halls, with smart phones and emails, and even face-to-face on television, in auditoriums, and in cafés. What will such changes require? In order to discuss e-voting, we need to remind ourselves how we got to this point.

# CHAPTER 3

## Our Unfinished Nation

• • •

*Remember that guy who gave up?*
*Neither does anyone else.*

—Unknown

After the original thirteen colonies won independence from the British Empire in 1781, what we call America did not exist yet. Very few conceived of the thirteen states as a nation—to this point, nations had usually been defined by monarchies or armed regimes—and the word "democracy" did not come into use until the next century, about 1850. A revolution like we had in 1776 involved guns, cannon, mobs, torches, and pitchforks—the usual props that accompany most revolutions. But in 1789, when the first Congress assembled and a constitution ratified by most of the original thirteen states existed, a nation was evident and began to function as such. We were a nation whose population numbered 3,929,214 in 1790, according to the U.S. census that included slaves. The point is that we were small, and we had no tradition as a democracy or as a nation. It was a brand-new approach.

No one at that time could have accurately predicted how great a nation we would become. Rebels who fought to break free of King George didn't often think about what would come next. The nation still had to be formed. The first (and so far only) National Constitutional Convention met from May 25, 1787 until September 17, 1787, when a final draft of the Constitution was approved. We believe and hope that a Second Constitutional Convention will be called where the nation's best minds can come together to make recommendations for revisions to the Constitution that will continue to protect our freedoms, maintain the separation of the branches of government, and allow for the evolution and expansion of democracy. In short, revisions to the Constitution could see the nation through another two centuries—preserved, protected and enhanced—in the same way the founders established a long-term legacy hundreds of years ago.

Our nation through its government, like a factory, produces safety, freedom, security, justice, and well-being for its citizens. But the machinery is old and needs maintenance. If we agree that repairs are needed, then we must make them so that the government of this great nation can achieve optimal functioning again. We need both inspiration to undertake this task and level-headed thinking about the mechanics of how a democracy can work best for the future for a hundred times more people than when it began. At the same time, we might, just might, create a model that other nations can adopt to spread democracy to places where people need to be free and functioning fully. We can still dream that everyone can achieve their full potential that our experiment and our experience will benefit others.

When large corporations begin to experience challenges, it is usually not due to lack of human talent. It is often the result of the business structures that initially created success getting out of step with the market forces that continued to evolve. We blame the people, but the outdated operations are often the underlying cause. Some businesses realize this, and in the corporate sense "amend their constitutions." They often can be successful again.

Too often when faced with significant change in the corporate world, employees feel powerless. Borrowing from the work of Christopher Avery, CEO of Partnerwerks (which studies responsibility within larger organizations), and applying it to our national situation, we feel that if our lives are to get better, then Congress must be the first one to change. We blame them. Too often we think something external must change for our lives to improve. But this is just a mental state that says someone else must change first before I can take resourceful action. In the corporate world, the excuse frequently heard is *that's just the way it is around here. Management has always operated this way and that's the culture we have so there is nothing I can do about it.* So we spend our precious resources coping with difficult situations rather than facing them directly and beginning to change them—because we need our jobs, but also because our interest is tied to the overall business's success.

We apply that same model to our government. We think we cannot do anything about the way we are governed because it's been in place now for over two hundred years. We must disabuse ourselves of this mindset. There is much voters have the power to change, and like the hypothetical corporation, we not only want to stay in business, we want to be successful.

Avery says we are hard-wired to avoid true ownership. All commentators, journalist, pundits, and politicos say that the only way we can fix any problem is for Congress to do something about it. In order to get a better result, we must contact our congressional representatives. Many books and articles that advocate for change in our system conclude with an instruction to take action—to create political action committees, write letters, email, and call our representatives. And, if this approach doesn't work, then we must elect a new representative during the next election cycle. Haven't we done all of that before? Then why are things still broken? We're still trying to manufacture Cadillacs in a factory tooled to make horse carriages.

In movies about the Old West, when the driver has been shot and the horses startled, the lives of passengers are in peril. Usually a brave passenger opens the stagecoach door and with pluck and determination makes his way to the driver's seat. We see a cliff and spinning spokes of the stagecoach's wheels before he makes it to the driver's seat, regains control, and reins in the steeds. Films and stories of the Old West contain many examples of brave people doing what needed to be done to bring about the results they desired. They didn't ask permission or seek a vote first. Today, individual action is muted in a population of hundreds of millions. The twenty-first-century version of action requires unified action of a sizeable majority. To change our current results, we must undertake a new way of thinking about how democracy works and our own role in it. We only need pull from our holster our most powerful weapon—our collective vote—to make change happen within our living constitution.

Avery shows how we respond when things go wrong. We get mired in our old coping mechanisms. He says our first instinct after we realize we have a role to play is to begin each statement with the phrase "I lack." We say, *I lack the knowledge, ability or experience to handle the challenge that faces me.* Actually, we learn mostly through trial and error and correcting our errors over and over. Our parents tell us not to touch the stove, but most of us do anyway. But then we learn, and it's real to us.

We always wish we knew back then what we know now. Collectively as a nation, we lack neither knowledge nor ability to make difficult changes. We have sufficient knowledge, power, and the right to call for a National Constitutional Convention to determine what change will look like. If you're not open to significant change in our governance, you are freed from reading farther.

> *The major challenges facing the United States today are not problems of policy, but problems of governance. Our system is broken because we have imposed policies from the center that should be decided locally. Making those centralized policies more "conservative" will not improve our system; in fact, that will likely make things worse by increasing support for a bad governance structure. And a good policy under a bad governance structure ultimately morphs into a bad policy.*
>
> —Leo Linbeck III, *The American Conservative*

## But What If Things Get Worse?

When we begin to feel trapped in a situation, we tend to avoid responsibility. Although everyone knew that slavery was an issue, we let the Civil War start because we could not agree collectively on responsibility for the problem. After a bloody conflict, the Constitution was changed.

People often fear change for no logical reason. When we fear change, we sometimes focus on an obligation to keep things from getting worse, rather than being innovative with solutions. If we say that we want a larger role in our governance, how can *we* do that? Our founders never intended for us to be fearful of our own power to bring about change. They embraced the risks and rewards inherent in a broad-based democracy.

We might think like this and tell ourselves:

*I feel I have the knowledge or ability, but I know too many others who make all the wrong decisions about their affairs. There is no way I can trust others to help fix this nation as well as I could.*

*My primary obligation is to keep things from getting worse for my family. Others are not as smart, as well-meaning as I am, nor do they have my largeness of vision. If we make these changes, how can I keep people who cannot even hold a job from having a larger role in my governance? They will act irresponsibly. They will vote to do away with taxes or raise mine. The best thing to do is leave things as they are. The problem is so big that I cannot possibly dare to think about taking positive action to change a system that could just as likely make things worse.*

The current solution that we try over and over remains that we all need to elect a better Congress—one that gets things done. But changing who is in Congress does not fix the underlying issue. Congressional dysfunction is a symptom rather than a cause.

Psychologists have studied trust issues and related issues for years. The simplest explanation is that the first time you trust a stranger and are disappointed or betrayed (scams are plentiful on the eleven o'clock news across the country), you don't ever want to trust strangers again. This is natural. This response protects us. Everyone who knocks on my front door wants something from me! Similarly, the Dunning-Kruger effect verified that incompetent people suffer from the belief that they are more capable than they are. All this is true. You may be thinking that this applies to the authors of this book! So be it.

We have to trust each other and believe in each other if we are to make a better nation with greater opportunity and provide the option for wider and more direct participation in our democracy. That's why we are in the bind we're in—deep mistrust of those who are different from us. Indeed, we have to protect ourselves, but to make everyone a villain robs us of the potential within ourselves and others.

On a longer scale, we are significantly different from those who lived in this country several hundred years ago. If we met them face-to-face and had an hour to talk, we would likely find that they would be mistrustful of us. Fortunately, they bequeathed to us a system that allows for change. Our fear is the main thing holding us back.

## What Can I Do About our Government?

Here's what *we* can do. Bottom line, we must embrace our role in shaping the Constitution. The Constitution was created to establish a republic, balance the power of the three branches, and establish the mandate to allow governance of a new nation. Changes to the Constitution were then and remain the key to guaranteeing our future. No one wants to destroy the Constitution, but it no longer matches the times we live in either.

Every two years, we elect a new Congress. We grumble that our choices among candidates are too limited, that the candidate doesn't fully reflect our views, and that they will be influenced by too many lobbyists. That's all possibly true. But then the real kicker is that they refuse to work out compromises between the parties in both houses of Congress. We constantly hear commentators and politicians talk about apathetic voters. If you go to a restaurant that provides slow service, lousy menu options, and poorly prepared food, you stop going (or submit a bad review on social media!). We think that's the way voters feel.

Too many voters now say, "What good can my one vote do?" The electorate almost stops voting between presidential elections, but it's not the fault of the individual. It's the fault of a system not updated in over two hundred years. No one physically stops large numbers of people from voting (or if they do, it's against the law), so the reason people don't vote in off-year elections is that they simply don't see the return benefit. The Fourth Branch will give people the opportunity between elections to have a direct impact on current issues. Ultimately, it will make them more likely to vote by making it easier.

Historically, citizens of this nation have achieved greatness over and over. We can do it again now. We cannot blame our politicians for this current situation, however. When we hear representatives and senators, it is through the filter of a news anchor or an opponent. We might see them on the House or Senate floor or asking questions as a member of a committee. But we don't see the lobbyists at work, the campaign donations, or the backroom deals that often set the stage for media drama.

In an age of transparency, Congress continues to be guilty of tucking special interest provisions into bills, making changes behind closed doors, and passing bills without reading them. What if a committee of voters could hold a hearing to question a senator or congressman the same way we see them fire questions at cabinet officers, CEOs, celebrities, or other powerful people? The United States is a republic and yet once we send an elected official to Washington, we begin to feel they no long act in our interests. Is this the candidate's fault, or the system we elect them to? We're not saying this is always true. We're saying it feels like our best interests don't always make it to the finish line.

*America is the first democratic nation-state, now more than two and a quarter centuries old. Our greatest triumphs are the eighteenth-century creation of our democratic republic, the nineteenth-century abolishment of slavery and the holding together of our union, and twentieth-century crushing of totalitarianism.*

—Stephen E. Ambrose (historian)

Tom Brokaw named the generation that fought World War II "the greatest generation." We too now have an opportunity to leave our mark on our nation for our children. Like Native Americans, we must incorporate the Seventh Generation principle attributed to Native Americans that admonishes us to consider how our actions will affect our descendents seven generations into the future. We can build a structure of governance to match the world we leave behind, and we can encourage a system that will be flexible when we're no longer around and yet again the country is different. We cannot always sit back and enjoy the ride others provided us. We must keep the vehicle in repair through good governance and just laws and wider opportunities for everyone. Our actions need to be the next sentence in a quote that a future historian will record. Imagine a future historian saying of the changes we will bring about:

"In 2016, all over America, groups of citizens began to talk about and think about changes to democracy and the governance of our nation. They formed a national town square using the model of Wikipedia. They created organizations to focus attention on changing the Constitution first. Then once they re-balanced the power structure, they began to help put laws in place to create a better society that has flourished down to our time."

We own a great heritage—both good and bad. Our job is to

improve it for ourselves *and* future generations. We have a duty to hand off our nation to the next generations so that they can thrive and prosper as well as we have. We can expand democracy inside the existing framework of our republic to allow the inclusion of voter input between elections with carefully thought-out extensions of our Constitution. We are not even halfway done with the possibilities of America.

## Ask Tough Questions

We must ask the tough questions—not just of politicians but of each other as well. We must rebuild the government we have into the more effective government we want. We must reset the bar to a higher standard for all of us and stop blaming others. We begin the way a therapist might begin an initial session—look inward first. We can start by asking ourselves:

*What is my role? Did I vote in the last election? Am I pleased with my life and its prospects? Do I want to change it? Do I believe my children will have all that I have had? Am I willing to make a concerted effort in that direction? Can I bear to join with others who don't share all of my views to help restructure this nation's governance?*

We believe your answer is yes, and there is nothing else we can do but make changes to the Constitution if we want to restore our nation to prosperity and leadership. Discussion of the Fourth Branch requires that we ask tough questions.

If we need an educated workforce to compete in the future, then why do so many states cut funding to schools and colleges? And why doesn't Congress step in to change this outcome? Where are our leaders? Voters, if we choose, can fill the leadership gap by becoming voter-leaders. We can set up new institutions that will allow the electorate to be able to put forth bills to both Congress and the president.

Who says we don't have the right or the ability to decide what our nation's priorities are in the area of non-international policy making? We do have the right.

Congress will not likely reform itself. Changing any system from the inside is always difficult. Our goal is to change the structure of government in such a way as to create a framework for voter input in a more direct way. Rather than force change directly on Congress, empowering voters will enable Congress to change on its own. Democracy must evolve in the twenty-first century to remain a viable way to get things done. Our politicians currently block each other at every turn. We will have to give ourselves the tools to step in to help but not take over—to vote, amend, and participate.

## Build a Nation the Way You Want It to Look

*The moral test of government is how that government treats those who are in the dawn of life, the children, those who are in the twilight of life, the elderly; and those in the shadows of life, the sick, the needy and the unemployed.*

—Hubert H. Humphrey

Why can't we have a nation where poverty is decreasing and education increasing? We only need the will to do it and joint action to make it happen. Is it easier to improve schools, or put a man on the moon? We've proven we can solve problems we set for the national agenda. The first step begins with a conversation with each other about making changes to the Constitution that would give the voter a seat at the table of politics, not just at election times but during times between formal elections when governing takes place. Could we do worse than the current scenario? Maybe things could be worse without democracy, but in America, we always look to achieve better. We believe in democracy but need to also believe in better democracy. Now let's look at what we could do.

We must be ambitious for future voters and ourselves. Special interest groups are ambitious! They lobby legislators all day long to get what they want. It's time for us to lobby all day long for ourselves. It's not about taking anything away from anyone else. There is more than enough to go around.

## We Have Only One Bullet Left in the Chamber—Our Vote

No matter a person's wealth, education, or status, a registered voter still has only a single vote. Together our votes can have a powerful effect. Your vote is the least-used tool in your home. It's time to take it out, shine it up, and carry it down the street to the ballot box. And take your neighbor with you when you go. We are not describing a revolution but an evolution and reformation of our governance. We want to install a new framework around our governance that will allow wider and deeper voter participation and influence.

The mission is not to destroy the government but to provide a plan for a hope and for a future for everyone. The plans laid out in this book will make our governance more representative, more effective, and more capable. The changes we will describe require you to vote and vote and vote until you obtain the future that belongs to you the way it's intended. We want all of us to be the change that does not give up, does not get pushed away, does not accept delays, and no longer accepts empty promises.

Who said our prisons must be filled to overflowing? Who said it's okay to promote children unprepared for the next grade? Who said we must give up hope for our children and ourselves to find better jobs or find ways to create them? Who says that the middle class must die a slow and agonizing death? If Washington doesn't produce the leaders we need to turn things around, then the voters will step up and lead ourselves.

We're not proposing a revolution or a deep and crazy change to the way we live, but rather an evolution. We are, however, suggesting that we change the focus on our priorities. Let's be honest. The rich are getting richer, the middle class is in decline, and the poor are getting poorer. We want a means to be able to adjust some governance patterns and give everyone more opportunity. We are proposing an additional level of government that provides a spot where we can clarify our thoughts as voters through legislative action. If this becomes a movement with many participants, then it cannot be turned aside or held back; the power of vote will be confirmed.

If we must engage in a letter writing campaign, let's write a letter to each other. In this letter, let's promise each other that we will make our votes count. Let's promise that we want to see the Constitution fulfilled and effective for everyone.

## We Must Not Believe in Magical Thinking About Congress

Most suggestions for how to achieve solutions for national problems require Congress to act differently. Granted that situation, let's focus on how changing that might actually occur.

*If Congress is unresponsive, restoring self-governance is impossible. But lawmakers will not reform themselves. Thus the critical first step in returning to self-governance is making congressional elections work—reconnecting the ballot box and the people's will. This is a difficult task, but not impossible. Primary elections are the key.*

—Leo Linbeck III, *The American Conservative*

Congress will not change itself. They cannot agree on most major matters and they would be very unlikely to give away any of their power. Voters must take a long hard look at themselves—young and old. If we continue doing what we're doing, we will keep getting what we're getting. A preacher once said about change that the first thing to do is make up your mind to change. Then you announce to your family and friends that you will change so that you accept accountability for the change. The third and final step is to expect a miracle! We do not expect that this book's ideas will rapidly be adopted. We hope that readers will give them serious thought and begin to believe in change.

*The greatest challenge to policymaking today is distrust. The American people distrust their government and Congress in particular. For their part, Washington policymakers seem to distrust the people. And almost as pressing for the new majority, the distrust that exists between grassroots conservative activists and elected Republican leaders can be particularly toxic.*

*Leaders can respond to this distrust in one of two ways. One option is the bare-knuckled partisanship that Senate Majority Leader Harry Reid has exhibited for the last eight years: twisting rules, blocking debate and amendments, and systematically disenfranchising hundreds of millions of Americans from political representation.*

*But this is no choice at all for the new Republican majority. First, contempt for the American people and the democratic process is something Republicans should oppose in principle. Second, our new Senate majority will be both ideologically diverse and temperamentally independent—unlikely to be as docile and partisan as Senate Democrats have been.*

—Mike Lee, senator from Utah, November 6, 2014

## Where Do We Go from Here?

The remainder of this book proposes changes that we can make to first give ourselves the tools that will achieve a different outcome—e-voting is one. If we don't secure electronic voting, then we have effectively tied one hand behind our back. You can dig a hole in your garden with a shovel with one hand tied behind your back, but it takes a long, long time. With one hand tied behind your back, can you prepare dinner, easily use your cell phone, or tie your shoes? We cannot move forward as a nation by continuing to use a ballot box only in a precinct only on the first Tuesday only in November. Horse and buggy days are over!

# CHAPTER 4

## E-voting—First Step for Transforming Democracy

• • •

*There's no reason to have a plan B because it distracts from plan A.*

—Will Smith

Our nation in the twenty-first century operates electronically and with more efficiency and effectiveness because of the tools that even school children have available—smart phones, computers, and tablets. Our democracy must be adapted to utilize these kinds of electronic tools to enable better governance and more inclusive voting. We must integrate today's electronic tools with our constitutional voting process. Enabling e-voting for elections using technology to manage registration and election results is the first step.

If John Adams or Thomas Jefferson could revisit us today, they would praise all of the technological and efficiency-oriented advances (telephone, television, Internet, and other communications) used in commerce, education, and government operations. Suppose they could sit in the galleries in the House of Representatives today. The process of making laws is similar to what they experienced. They would feel at home and see that the Constitution operates as they intended.

There were about four million inhabitants of the United States in 1790. Now we have over 325 million citizens, or about eighty-five times greater population. And since women and African Americans could not vote then, the number of eligible voters is more than 160 times greater than in 1790. Additionally, since a much higher portion of the population were presumably children (under voting age) then, the number of voters today could be closer to 200 times larger. How can we continue to set up an adequate number of polling locations to accommodate an ever-expanding modern democracy? We will fall short in our attempt to maintain our republic if we keep doing it this way when we know the technology is sorely out of date.

We need to re-examine how we vote, realizing that the introduction of e-voting touches on the core of the electoral process—casting and counting votes. If we want to utilize e-voting, we will need to modify the Constitution to allow e-voting. Currently, states have the right to control elections. Does this still make sense? Our Constitution handled elections with the tools available in the eighteenth century. Therefore, states were responsible for setting up and tallying elections mainly because the federal government had no mechanism for doing that. We are the tenants and caretakers of our republic, our democracy. Adams, Jefferson, and all the other founders never envisioned the availability of the tools we have now. Elections should be handled at the national level in a uniform, fair, and accessible manner.

> *I shall not die without a hope that light and liberty are on steady advance.*
>
> —Thomas Jefferson to John Adams, 1821

## The Voting Patchwork

The Constitution bestows on states the right and responsibility for holding elections for senators and representatives. Article 1 Section 4 of the Constitution, called the "Elections Clause," describes the primacy of states in the voting process. "The times, places and manner of holding elections for Senators and Representatives, shall be prescribed in each state by the legislature thereof; but the Congress may at any time by law make or alter such regulations, except as to the places of choosing Senators." Over the years, this procedure produced a patchwork of voting methods. Historically, some localities tried to restrict voting to some groups even after the passage of the Fifteenth Amendment, which prohibits the denial of the right to vote based on race, color, or previous condition of servitude.

As businesses mature, they standardize their processes in order to maintain efficiency. Government agencies over time move from *ad hoc* processes and procedures to formally defined, repeatable steps in their operations. For example, when a president leaves office, the Secret Service has a set of protocols to follow to set up the security for the former president's new residence and his family. Each transition gets handled in the same way every time. That's what e-voting would do. Wherever a person lives in the nation, they would see the same procedures over and over again when voting. If an improvement is made, it will be reflected at every polling precinct or, if e-voting is implemented, across every device.

The protection and expansion of voting rights has been, and continues to be, a strong thread throughout our nation's history. We have a duty to maintain the ability of citizens to be able to vote. Putting voting rights in the hands of a federal agency and providing consistent, accessible e-voting could close the chapter on this issue once and for all. Anyone who qualifies and wishes to vote could have that access consistently and without artificial barriers. The patchwork of state laws could be rescinded. When you move your residence, you must register in your new location by a certain date to be able to vote. E-voting administered at the national level would only require that you update your residence by logging into your account, the way you already do for your bank, your driver's license, and so many other things.

To move to e-voting would require changing the Constitution, passing other laws in Congress to regulate how states conduct elections, and making changes to state constitutions and laws.

## Types of E-voting and Requirements for E-voting

Voting has a set of established and accepted requirements. First of all, a vote must be secret—no one should be able to see how anyone else voted. Second, if a recount or some other audit is required, the votes need to be in a form that makes that process work properly and with a degree of transparency. Third, the parts of the system must be secure and the security of the system needs to be auditable as well. The biggest hurdles to Internet voting involve security and cyber attack. Lastly, and not so obvious, the loser of an election must believe that they actually lost the election. There cannot be any doubt that all the votes got counted and counted correctly. There needs to be confidence in the system.

Where e-voting exists currently, there are four primary variations:

Punch-card voting systems: Many precincts utilize punch cards
that are scanned into a vote-tabulating device. The voter knows
immediately that their vote was secret and counted.
Optical scanning systems: A second system utilizes optical scanning.
This consists of pencil-marked paper, electronic ballot markers,
and digital pens.
Direct-recording electronic (DRE) systems: This system most often
consists of a touch screen (a benefit to vision-impaired voters,
enabling them to vote without assistance). The votes are stored on
a removable memory card and/or printed summary.
Internet voting system: This would allow voting from home, office,
mobile device, a polling precinct, or other public location such as
a library. This is the preferred method most voters would like to
see but also the system where meeting voting requirements will
be the greatest challenge. For purposes of our discussion, this is
the system we advocate at the national level, but e-voting using
the Internet presents the greatest challenge to achieving a secure,
verifiable system.

## 2012 Presidential Election

From all over the nation on Election Day in 2012, reports of the
inadequacy of the means to cast a simple ballot flooded the news.
Voting locations in the Northeast affected by Hurricane Sandy were
not open and no information was available designating alternate voting
sites. Scanning devices in Ohio did not work. Places that could accept
email votes were overwhelmed. Understaffed locations caused voters
to have to wait in long lines, and some voters cast ballots late into
the night. In the Seventh District of Virginia, a well-prepared district
where the authors live, voters experienced some delay but nothing
extreme. Across the nation, these anomalies were not necessarily
widespread or uniform but, nonetheless, they represent problems that
are systemic rather than random. In a sense, we stand in line wearing
a powdered wig, stockings, three-cornered hat, and shoes with bright
brass buckles because at the moment of putting pencil to paper to cast

a vote it actually puts my hand into the hand of those who forged the method of voting in use today. The act of voting is a great privilege and a cherished heritage, but we need to update the methodology of voting.

What Lewis P. Lapham, editor of *Harper's Magazine* for twenty-eight years and a respected political writer, said of political campaigns applies to municipalities administering voting precincts. Local governments don't "favor the voters with the gratitude and respect owed to their standing as valuable citizens participating in the making of such a thing as a common good." Admittedly, it would be hard to individually acknowledge the 124 million who voted in the 2012 presidential election. But the process will continue to be flawed until our procedures are updated through a constitutional amendment enabling electronic voting. This would require that the nation's election process be under the control of the federal government.

There were enough problems in 2012, however, for President Obama to appoint a commission on May 21, 2013 to review the voting problems that occurred on Election Day. President Obama said, as reported by Rachel Rose Hartman, on that day when he announced the commission:

> *As I said in my State of the Union Address, when any American, no matter where they live or what their party, is denied the right [to vote] simply because too many obstacles stand in their way, we are betraying our ideals. We have an obligation to ensure that all eligible voters have the opportunity to cast their ballots without unwarranted obstructions or unnecessary delay.*

Regardless of the findings of that commission, it is time to change the Constitution so that all voting at the national level—and perhaps even for all levels of government, including local elections—be administered by the federal government. This is a states' rights issue and will be a long, hard fight to get this changed, but it's the change we need. Ashley Southall in an article in *The New York Times* said:

*Voting rights advocates have welcomed the creation of the panel, spurred by long lines and voting problems in the 2012 elections that experts say disproportionately affected poor and minority voters, who are traditionally Democratic constituencies. But the groups are tempering their expectations until they see whether the panel is effective.*

*The executive order creating the commission pointed to problems faced by members of the military, overseas voters, voters with disabilities and voters with limited English proficiency and special needs. It listed the training of poll workers, issues with polling centers and voting machines, the management of voter rolls, ballot simplicity and overseas balloting among several suggested areas of study.*

## Reasons to Move to E-voting

1. E-voting makes voting easier. Voters could vote from wherever they are.
2. E-voting improves the ability of those with disabilities to cast votes.
3. With a voting window of a few days, or a week, nearly everyone who wants to vote will be able to do so. Government employees in the military or diplomatic corps will be able to vote without absentee ballots. People on vacation or working out of town during the voting window will be able to cast their ballots.
4. It will demonstrate that we, as a nation, think voting is so important that it should be made accessible to everyone who is eligible.
5. E-voting makes voting more accurate when tallied since there will never be manual counting.
6. It reduces interruptions to schools because they won't close on election days.
7. E-voting establishes more uniform processes on Election Day

because states are responsible for running elections, which has created a patchwork of processes across the country.

8. An e-voting interface can provide a bilingual version and display pictures of the candidates for face recognition.

9. E-voting demonstrates that we can keep our democracy in step with the times.

## E-voting Difficult to Achieve

Across the country and around the world, municipalities are either utilizing a form of e-voting or investigating the possibility. From a user and usability viewpoint, Internet e-voting will be a significant improvement. But the challenges researchers have found make most Internet security experts believe voting over the Internet has significant challenges. Some of the commonly cited challenges are:

1. E-voting is more difficult to implement than Internet banking. If you make a payment through your bank account, the bank knows who the payment is from and who the payment is going to. With e-voting you know who gets the payment (the candidate) but you can't tell who sent it (for audit or verification).

2. E-voting makes it hard to insure chain of custody of votes if a recount is required (who has the original data).

3. If an election gets hacked, it may be months before it's discovered. Awareness of a hacked system is not usually uncovered until after the fact.

4. There is also a chance of an "insider attack" by someone who works for an election agency or for a company that provides the election equipment or software (although this is already a challenge with current methods).

5. Voting over the Internet with well-known protocols invites interference.

6. Setting up a help system is a problem of extreme complexity with all the variation of devices a voter may be using.

7. Many personal devices already contain malware that may subvert voting on the user's end.

8. Systems developed by private companies who claim to have

solved the problems of e-voting will have to be rigorously tested over years to determine if they are truly secure.

9. No system yet can be completely secure. There are always vulnerabilities.

Even though Internet e-voting will present very difficult technological challenges, Internet e-voting is currently the most user-friendly way to conduct voting. Manual voting administered mostly in churches and schools on only one day of the year during limited hours puts a moat around fuller participation in our democratic republic. Voting is a drawbridge that is let down generally every other year when the townspeople are allowed inside the castle to be heard and then dismissed to go back to work. We've had enough of this.

## A Barn Doesn't Fall Down All at Once

Decay springs from natural causes—wind, weather, neglect, and time. A significant number of civilizations, empires, and cities that once thrived no longer exist or did not pass along the heritage they once had. Some we know from the structures or art they left behind. We don't always know the cause of their decline. Few of them ended overnight. It took hundreds of years for the Roman Empire to finally succumb to roaming armies of Vandals, Goths, and Huns. Every civilization and system tends to decline. Read the British-American historian Niall Ferguson for insight into this process for modern civilization and commerce.

The barn metaphor is an idea that came from driving a beautiful stretch of US 259 going from Virginia into West Virginia. Because of the lack of flat land, many houses and farm structures dot the land along the road. Barns in various stages of decay pop up from time to time.

The decay scenario goes something like this. The purpose of the barn simply no longer exists. It may once have held animals or feed or hay—something used in the course of farm activities. But the process changed and the need for the barn no longer exists. The farmer doesn't want to tear it down because there might be a future need for it. Some of the farms are not active any more. Most of the barns that catch the eye have little or no paint left on them—usually just bare clapboards. Tin roofs never painted turn to rust along with the nails holding them on before the sheets get twisted or blown off. Wind rips some panels off and the barn looks like a smile with a gap tooth. Many have vines growing up them, tugging the boards down. Finally they begin to cave in section by section.

Institutions made by man are the same way. We must maintain our democracy—keep the roof in repair and keep it in constant use; paint the siding. Voter participation declines in part because our lives and habits change, but our method of voting has stayed the same. The barn of our democracy needs repair. It needs a new roof. Let's run some wiring to the barn so we can have light in there. Voting is a core structure in our democracy, and we need to revitalize it. Internet e-voting is the first step.

## Partial Electronic Voting Already Taking Hold

To various degrees, municipalities already utilize some elements of electronic voting, e-voting. Every precinct tabulates ballots marked with pencil on paper, utilizing optical electronic scanning. Some localities have already begun to use a form of e-voting. Nevada County, California, has adopted eLect® software for its elections. The population of Nevada County is relatively small, so it will be a good test of this kind of system in a real election. Corporations rely on electronic voting to tabulate votes at annual meetings. Countless organization rely on e-voting to avoid the cost of a paper election. Localities and private enterprises are already solving the technical problems of e-voting. From the website of everyonecounts.com:

> *Our eLect® Electronic Voting and eLect® Telephone Voting options give remote citizens more convenient, secure, and reliable ways to participate in an election from any location with telephone or Internet access. These voting methods increase accessibility for military and overseas voters and voters with disabilities, and are fully compliant with—and exceed the expectations of—*

*United States federal laws such as the Help America Vote Act (HAVA) and the Uniformed and Overseas Citizens and Absentee Voting Act (UOCAVA), as well as similar laws established in countries outside of the U.S.*

We must not be discouraged as we explore how best to implement Internet e-voting. Failures of invention haunted Thomas Edison, who famously said, "I have not failed. I've just found 10,000 ways that won't work." Our nation believes in success through failure, when failing means that you are trying. Every failure masks the success waiting to be exposed. We must look beyond any systems that have failed, or fallen out of date, and find the ones that will succeed.

Who in 1900 believed man would one day fly over the ocean? Whenever a number of groups begin to work to solve a problem, a solution cannot be far behind. Every morning millions of citizens go to their job or avocation to discover new ideas, create new products, or find ways to make a process more efficient. Our nation resembles a reactor where we collide with each other through commerce and ideas. We give off an amazing energy that creates new kinds of communications, remedies for diseases, and new inventions. E-voting stands as just another challenge to be solved through our natural ingenuity and drive.

**Internet E-voting Manhattan Project**

To achieve Internet e-voting so that it meets all of the requirements of voting will take a huge concerted effort from a lot of directions. Just as the nation created the Manhattan Project during World War II for the development of the atomic bomb, we could pull together top talent from across the nation and even the world to create a working Internet e-voting system. Nothing is impossible in America, yet. We can never lose our nerve or courage or desire to travel to new frontiers.

## Brunelleschi's Dome

Perhaps a prize for the solution to the Internet e-voting dilemma could be created. A successful example of a difficult problem resolved is called Brunelleschi's Dome. Construction began in 1296 on the Cathedral of Santa Maria del Fiore in Florence, Italy. In August 1418, the *Arte della Lana* (the Wool Guild of Florence) announced a competition for the design of the dome that would complete the church. Lorenzo Ghiberti and Filippo Brunelleschi, two goldsmiths, were the primary competitors and named co-architects and builders. During the project, Brunelleschi feigned illness and Ghiberti took over direction but admitted he could not complete the work. It was Brunelleschi's way of making sure that he actually got a chance to solve the problem by himself. But what does this have to do with e-voting? If a genius could be found to build a dome that even today remains mysterious—no one is certain how Brunelleschi actually did it—then we can find a group of people or one individual who can design an Internet e-voting solution that meets all of the requirements. Brunelleschi relied on his natural intelligence and insight, but he also needed an opportunity. We have a moment in time where that opportunity is opening. Mathematical tools for calculating stresses were centuries in the future. Masons completed the dome without the use of interior scaffolding. Sometimes the insight arrives first and the science catches up later.

As we will argue throughout this book, our nation contains a large number of very, very smart people. In the past, some of them might have been called geniuses. Another way of thinking about this is that the larger our country grows, the more people with innovative ideas we should have. All of the answers can't come from Congress alone. Professors from Rice University advised Travis County, Texas, (Austin), on requirements for a new voting system they were planning. We have pockets of academics who, if put together, could create requirements and designs for e-voting that would meet the requirements of secrecy, accuracy, and auditability. Perhaps engineers from private companies could also provide input by designing semiconductors or other equipment that only works for elections to keep them secure. The world will be newer tomorrow than it is today. We just need to make it so. Once Bruneschelli was awarded the opportunity, he made his contractors and artists innovate to meet the need. Perhaps

51

government and private enterprise can create a Bell Laboratories of the twenty-first century for e-voting. We can make the sky come down closer than it is.

Additionally, if we want the convenience of e-voting and the infrastructure to support it, we will have to make other changes to the Constitution and to laws. Suppose that we reduce the demands on our voting systems in the future? Not all officials would be required to be elected on Tuesday after the first Monday in November. A lot of local elections could be handled on other months of the year. This would enable us to better utilize staff we will need to administer elections. Elections could be held during election "windows" so that voters could vote on weekends and at times when they are not so rushed. By the official Election Day, all voting would have to be concluded. Spreading out elections would save money and better utilize election resources. It is a given that more people would participate. The results would be kept secret and all results announced at the same time.

Perhaps not as exciting as staying up all night to see the results announced, but maybe more fair and democratic.

## We Cannot Live in Fear of Fraud

We live in a world of "e-danger." We hear about it every day. A system or individual's computer is hacked every hour. We also put ourselves at risk every time we get behind the wheel on the road. But the benefits of driving outweigh whatever dangers are inherent from driving. Internet e-voting is the same. One of the biggest fears is that someone evil wants to run the nation or the Congress so they develop a way to forge ballots electronically that leaves no audit trail. We could then lose our hard-won democracy. Such an argument believes that electronic voting cannot be kept secret, secure, and accountable. Some point out that to make e-voting auditable, then secrecy must be compromised. The problem of e-voting seems to some, at this moment, an intractable, unsolvable problem.

We've already mentioned a number of examples of intractable problems. Yet a man did walk on the moon. We cannot avoid or shy away from creating a solution because we think it's too difficult. That sounds like an excuse. The vitality of the democratic process depends on keeping voting up-to-date. Difficult problems are put in our path to keep us on our toes. This could be our generation's challenge, similar to cracking the Enigma code of Nazi Germany. Maybe some corporations or philanthropists could combine resources to create a twenty-first-century Bletchley Park where the problem could be solved. There may be teams in separate locations around the nation working on the problem in competition with each other, a series of Bletchley Parks. There could be confidential Internet e-voting conventions where different teams show off their progress to other teams. Ideas could be exchanged and out of that potent mix could come the solutions we will need to ensure the continual progress of our republic, not just in e-voting, but in many areas. Several private corporations market solutions already around the world for similar processes. The solution may already exist; we just need to test it, adapt it, and embrace it.

## E-voting Will Revitalize the Nation

We are in favor of e-voting. We are in favor of making it easier to vote. We are in favor of not waiting in line to vote. We are in favor of allowing more people to vote. We are in favor of more registered voters. Before we can begin to tackle some of the large problems facing us, we must enable Internet e-voting in its widest application.

Beyond the operation of Internet e-voting, to be discussed in the next chapter, e-voting will need to be accepted by the electorate. Some voters will need to be trained how to use a computer to enter their vote. Media and the commentators who focus almost exclusively on the problems and challenges we face will now have an opportunity to promote e-voting and offer their talents to the transition to e-voting. We will need a national civics lesson and training to show how to vote electronically. We must expect a transition phase over several years. E-voting may sound like an idea we just say yes to, but there will be hurdles getting millions of people to vote this way for the first time. But if we can build the Hoover Dam, the San Francisco Bay Bridge, and the Panama Canal, then this should be easily within our reach and not something to be avoided. E-voting offers the same kind of benefit as a bridge or canal by providing a more efficient way to get to a destination.

## Summary

E-voting is so clear and so basic that it demands a permanent, far-reaching solution. The way we cast our votes can be improved upon and changed by creating a plan and implementing that plan through legal means already established. But it requires a Constitutional amendment, which means this change will require a lot of effort, since amendments are few and far between. But if a significant majority of the population wants a specific, identifiable change, the change can be implemented through focused efforts. E-voting has the potential to allow us to change the governance of our world and to do so from the comfort of a swanky coffee shop or from the Spartan surrounding of a homeless shelter in a church basement.

# CHAPTER 5

## Setting Up Internet E-voting

• • •

*Always listen to experts. They'll tell you what can't be done, and why. Then do it.*

—Robert A. Heinlein, *Time Enough for Love*

The United States can no longer ignore the need to implement some form of electronic voting, preferably Internet-based e-voting. If nothing else, the millennial generation will implement it in another generation anyway whether we want to or not. It would serve our democracy much better to implement it as soon as possible. But Internet e-voting will be a very difficult thing to implement because of the need for secrecy and the ability to audit or recount the results.

Many will want to wait because the discussions too often will devolve into exchanges of differences of opinion due to all the unknowns around e-voting. It is likely that an expert will be found to justify any reason for or against. We cannot uncover the obstacles until we decide to accumulate the resources to investigate and find a solution. The reason for so much contention arises from two sources—the fear of fraud and the possible loss of power if all groups had easy access to vote. The issue falls into the camp of raw emotion rather than rational consideration of how to make it happen. While we cannot cover every possible scenario, we will present an option we think could work.

*History is a relentless master. It has no present, only the past rushing into the future. To try to hold on is to be swept away.*

—John Fitzgerald Kennedy

The problem with discussions around the issues of electronic voting brings to mind what occurs during a telecast of a presidential debate. Whichever candidate begins to address the last question constantly drags into the answer other points the candidate wishes to make that may be unrelated to the question he or she was asked. Discussions of electronic voting will raise questions about whether the states or the federal government should have the right or responsibility to administer elections. Another concern is if a system can handle the load when a presidential election, congressional elections, state and local elections all fall on the same day? How can we prevent fraud? How can we keep voting results secret? These are important questions. Discussions of electronic voting must be structured in a way that the issues are dealt with in a linear fashion.

Not only does the average voter lack clarity into how to set up e-voting, but experts are uncertain about how Internet voting can be made secure and, at the same time, easy to use.

A nation that put a man on the moon should be able to overcome the logistics and challenges of establishing electronic voting. We first must harness the collective will to do it. Although this book cannot say what the final features of the system will be, we can lay out a possible path. If we can create a Constitutional amendment to establish electronic voting, then the logistics of how it would operate and how it would be administered can be figured out later. First, we must simply make a decision to establish electronic voting or not. Initially, there could be a vote by some state legislatures to find a way to conduct secure Internet e-voting and then later present the findings to Congress and the nation. Alternatively, Congress could also fund an effort to discover how to implement e-voting. Private industry and private foundations might take the lead, especially if it is incentivized into a competition of ideas.

We cannot propose a Constitutional amendment that says, "We will have Internet e-voting when we figure out how to implement it securely." We might never get agreement that a system is secure enough to use.

## Build One or More Working Prototypes at the State Level

A new era of citizen-based ideas on politics has arrived, and we have technology in part to thank for that. We are no longer dependent just on electing a president with a unique vision who alone is tasked with leading us forward with change. Because our country has grown so much, everyone is tasked to update our democracy. Frankly, we live in feeble times when ideas as simple as raising the minimum wage can be blocked by no more people than can fit on a pleasure cruise boat that sails the Potomac at night. With Internet e-voting and the Fourth Branch, every voter can become a direct legislator of new ideas that may turn into laws, working in tandem with elected officials who will spend more time in their home districts than they do in Washington, D.C.

Before these changes can happen, several things need to occur. Maybe this idea has enough worth that leaders of a single state prompted by their voters would create a prototype Internet e-voting system to test alongside its current voting apparatus to discover how e-voting could work best. Some localities are already doing this. Perhaps Congress would fund a national prototype. Either way, only when Internet e-voting has been proven to work can it advance beyond the pages of a book or into a wider arena. No idea without action has ever accomplished anything. Coal must have a furnace before it can give off heat.

The process of establishing e-voting could become a new model for how future laws can be made. Laws meant for the nation could be tested in a prototype before even going to Congress for a vote. Or a law could be made to cover a few states at first and then rolled out to the rest of the nation when it reaches its final form. What if the Affordable Care Act could have been passed and tested in a few states to work out all the details before rolling it out to the nation?

## Internet E-voting Could Be Administered by the Federal Government

Voting oversight by a federal bureau provides the best way to protect and manage voter rights. State legislatures have historically handled voter rights very inconsistently. The federal government in the twenty-first century has the most complete records and is the logical place to maintain voter security and records. People move freely from one city and state to another. Residency tests exist to match benefits to taxpayers of a state, such as in-state college tuition. It makes sense to maintain one national database for everyone's records, the way we already do with Social Security, for example. One possibility is to actually extend the Social Security Administration database to encompass e-voting. A small benefit of such a system is that if a voter moved shortly before an election, their new precinct could easily be aligned to the change in address.

Centrally managing voting would almost certainly save money in the long run. Currently, localities must buy and maintain equipment and supplies to run elections that occur usually every other year, or even annually in states like Virginia. Each locality makes its own decisions and maintains its own records. There may be costs to change the current system, such as localities that might have to make available some computers for voters to use during elections at public places such as libraries or set up terminals at former voting precincts. Community organizations that already advocate for voting access might also take this on as one of their services. There would ultimately be a huge cost savings by moving to e-voting regardless of short-term expense.

It makes good sense for the federal government to operate all electronic voting in order to make the option of a Fourth Branch of government possible. In other words, even if our current electorate does not want some degree of direct popular democracy, we could create the option in case future generations decide they want it, and it would be a necessary component for a Fourth Branch of government. It is important that we anticipate what future generations might need by giving them the tools to adapt.

## Where Does This Leave Local Elections?

If the federal government takes over running elections, then it will likely have to administer state and local elections as well. Before saying that the task would be too big to handle, we should consider all of the tools we already have to perform tests and verifications. Everyone has in mind the failure of HealthCare.gov when it struggled initially, but that was a plan poorly executed. We would recommend that an amendment to the Constitution allow for elections to occur during a window of days or weeks to accommodate all of the elections that need to take place. In fact, that window could be completely opened for locales to decide. The voting window could end with the traditional first Tuesday in November Election Day. But a longer window for placing a vote would allow for people who are not able to vote on a specific day to be able to vote and spread out the load of voting demand over several days, or even weeks. In any case, results would not be announced until the final votes are cast. With advances in hardware and Internet speed, it is quite possible that by the time we implement electronic voting there will be enough capacity for every election to occur and every citizen to vote on the same Election Day, or during the same window.

The most likely scenario would be to allow state and local elections to take place on days other than the first Tuesday in November. Past laws established these rules and future laws can adjust the rules. Voters and regulations can adapt to any future changes if we establish a framework that encourages that.

## Individual Voter Accounts

If we pass an amendment to the Constitution to allow electronic voting, many details could be sorted out by those who build the system. Assuming it was not part of the Social Security system as we've already suggested, each voter would have an account with all basic information stored there. The voter rolls from each state could be imported, but because of the various record differences among states there could be some complexity to doing it this way. When someone applies for a Social Security number, their date of birth is recorded. That would be the trigger that determines when a voter's record flips so that individual may log on to vote. Once the voting system is in place, the Social Security system would send that data over. Each year a person would still be required to re-verify their voter account, the same way banks and financial agencies often require customers logging in to re-verify their information.

A voter record would hold basic information such as name, address, email, Social Security number, and security questions for account access. In any case, a voter would have to verify their voting account, but ultimately voter registration is automatic based on the Social Security flag. An account may be blocked later due to a legal situation such as incarceration or felony conviction. Pardons could unlock an account.

## How Votes Could Be Recorded and Security Established

Voting within each election cycle would be a three-stage process. It would work the same way as a realtor gets entry to a house she wants to show a client. The voter does not own the house, but is allowed access this one time. The voter enters their user ID and password, which allows access to the key stored inside the "real estate lockbox." The Bureau of Voting and Elections (created as a result of the amendment) will email the account holder a randomly generated key and pin good for this single election cycle only. If the voter doesn't have the second key and pin, they will be able to request a new one but will be logged off the system automatically at that point with instructions on how to retrieve the second key and pin. This is the author's hypothetical prototype of how all of this would work. After passage of an amendment to create e-voting, a suitable methodology would be vetted, tested, and put in place. We can only propose the idea.

Traditional keys are manufactured with a series of grooves on each side. A warded lock is a type of lock that uses a set of obstructions, or wards, to prevent the lock from opening unless the inserted key has grooves that match the key's wards. The second step is that the notches on the key fit the tumblers or pins in the lock. These two actions provide the holder of the key entry into the building. The second key and pin must match what is assigned and stored for this voter's account. This works as the "ward" on the lock. The voter and hence potential hacker cannot generate the second key and pin.

The screen for entering votes is active now, but no vote has been recorded. The voter marks the electronic ballot. Those selections are encrypted on the "token" for this account for this one day only.

There will be a final step to cast and record a vote. When the voter enters the second key and pin, the system issues a voting "token." The voter does not know that they are using a token, however. The token actually becomes the voter. By using tokens, there will be no way to track how any individual voted, only confirm that they did vote. The token registers the vote of the individual voter. The token is a randomly generated voting object that holds a citizen's election choices once a vote is cast. Tokens will be saved for recount purposes. The token could contain an encryption key that prevents anyone but the final depository from seeing the candidate choices, and the tabulating system could not identify an individual voter. A mirror token could at the same time be sent to an independent audit depository so that if a recount is required, those records should mirror the actual results. We are not computer science experts, but we believe that a team of experts could work out these details satisfactorily.

For the final step, each voter would have received at some point a final pin code via text message, email, or by calling on landline phone to an automated system to retrieve a pin. To have your vote recorded, you will enter the phone number associated with the text and must enter that pin. At that point the voter's selection, recorded on an anonymous token, goes to the tabulating system. We cannot be sure how this would work in a technology-based solution, but this is the concept we offer. The voter would only perform these actions once a year, and it is reasonable that these several steps would still save time since a trip to a polling precinct is no longer required.

It is important to understand as well that the interface voters would actually "see" when they use this security technology would be very simple and user-friendly, accessible to people with disabilities, and easy to understand. The technology would mainly be working behind the interface to ensure security.

If a person logs on to vote, but for some reason has to cancel before they cast their vote, the token would be destroyed. If a voter receives a token and uses the token to vote, their account will be marked as "voted." Once a voter hits the final "submit" button by sending a security access code back to the system, their voting is over until the next election. Additionally, voters will receive an automatically generated text showing their vote was recorded, but showing no details. The text message is a simple reminder and confirmation that one's vote has been cast. Features similar to these have been established by financial institutions and may only need to be adapted for use in electronic voting. Only if the proper security to maintain the secrecy of a vote could be developed should an email to the voter's account display how their vote was recorded, but a text acknowledgement that the vote was recorded would be reasonable and possible even with current technology.

There might be several steps behind the scenes so that a voter's token goes to one central computer where it is checked for viruses or tampering before being forwarded to the official database for recording and tallying the votes. These few paragraphs cannot do justice to all the intricacies of Internet e-voting. Such an implementation would create many commissions, reports, and books to cover the subject. We can only hit the highest spots and begin the conversation and emphasize in the strongest possible terms that it is very possible to create a solution using current technology.

The main point is that security concerns are *not* the correct reason to resist e-voting. E-voting would expand the franchise by eliminating all of the traditional barriers to voting: distance, time of day, work, and even barriers like race or gender, which theoretically don't exist anymore. It would enhance accessibility for individuals with disabilities. E-voting is color blind, gender blind, and gives the ultimate access to everyone freely. Our democracy is sadly overdue for such an energizing injection of the people's voting participation.

## Customer Service and Fraud Monitoring

Customer service could hypothetically be a challenge, fielding millions of requests around election week. Voters will be able to conduct test votes with their account up to two weeks prior to the election window. If a person forgets their password, they will receive a new one the same way banks and credit card companies handle these requests. Overall training for both users and system administrators will need to be done months in advance. Test areas—some call them virtual playgrounds, where voters can practice voting to see how the system works—not only trains the user but also builds trust in the validity of the system. Testing of all aspects of the system will be necessary.

Fraud protection and other security features will be built into the voting system. The federal government will be fortunate to be able to draw on the experience of financial and other institutions' successes in these areas, where technology has had to keep abreast of repeated security challenges. For example, banks store the IP (Internet Protocol) address of every computer that logs on to an account. If a customer uses the same device each time, the bank is not suspicious. But if a bank account is accessed by a different device, security questions pop up. Banks and financial institutions spend a great deal of money to stay ahead of fraud. Electronic voting needs to be as safe.

Another safety factor is simply the large number of votes that we cast during an election. It would be very difficult to steal enough accounts to sway an election. Plus wide-scale attacks would trigger alarms. Lastly, a simple CAPTCHA (Completely Automated Public Turing test to tell Computers and Humans Apart) entry would prevent large-scale attacks. (A "CAPTCHA" is a box usually near the bottom of the screen where you're entering data that shows a set of numbers and/or letters in a blurry format so that only a human could decipher what they are. The person entering data then types the correct sequence into the "CAPTCHA" box area.) Of course, hackers continually try to find ways to get into systems every hour of every day. Maintaining system integrity is a constant battle of cyber security monitoring and controlling. One good thing about a national system is that it could be taken offline between elections so that hackers could not practice getting in. The interface, the front end where users update their accounts, is online all the time so that updates can occur whenever necessary. But parts of a system can be separated to minimize potential intrusions.

History has myriad examples in America and in other countries of elections and ballots being tampered with. Technology actually promises to help us implement a more efficient and more secure voting system.

## Voters Without Computers or Smart Devices

Every voter must log in and update or confirm their existing account information prior to voting. Voters who use a friend's computer or public computer receive immediate confirmation on their screen just like everybody else. You don't have to own your device to vote.

Electronic voting will make voting accessible to more citizens. People with disabilities or those who may lack transportation on Election Day to polling places may be able to cast votes with electronic devices. Volunteers who currently pick up voters and take them to voting precincts may be able to take a device to them instead. A disruptive technology is one that displaces an established technology and shakes up an industry, or it could be a way of doing something completely differently. For example, the personal computer displaced the typewriter and the way we communicate. E-voting would be disruptive in a good way. This technology brings the ballot box to the voter. Friends and family could assist others in voting.

Although voters must answer security questions before voting, someone could theoretically ask that person for the information and then cast votes for their own preferences, thereby in effect "stealing" a vote. This is where a federal bureau of elections can develop guidelines for how people can behave when assisting others in voting (we already have those for poll workers now) and for how campaigns can interact with voters. But it is not a reason by itself to avoid the implementation of e-voting. Who would have enough time to uncover all the security questions from a significant number of voters and then enter them into a system to be able to cast votes for their preferred candidate in enough quantity to sway an election?

## Conclusion

To ensure a better democracy for future generations and ourselves, we need to approve and implement electronic voting. That's a first step. Then we will need a sort of Manhattan Project to bring in the best talent to create the best system possible. Imagine top corporations such as Cisco, Apple, or Hewlett-Packard along with universities loaning some of their top talent for a year to design and build the best system we could get. Or imagine the federal government creating a competition with a large prize to design and build a prototype. Very little is beyond the grasp of our nation's best minds. We are awash in genius and can apply it to solve problems.

Fear of this change and of possible fraud must be set aside. No one can guarantee that votes are not bought from voters who cast ballots in the traditional way. Making the system available to more people will negate possible fraud, and technology has already proven that it can help eliminate fraud.

We, as a nation, must do what Ray Bradbury, the science fiction writer, told us to do to be successful. "We must continually jump off cliffs and build our wings on the way down." Each generation has a duty to build the wings that lift the next generation. Duty exists to remind us and extol us to always strive for the next goal. Electronic voting will have the same effect as plugging a lamp into a socket and turning it on—we can thereby illumine the world again with a beacon.

# CHAPTER 6

## Retiring the Electoral College

• • •

*When you're finished changing, you're finished.*

—Benjamin Franklin

Every four years, we vote for a president and vice-president. The process consists of more than voters going to the polls and placing a mark beside the candidates' names. That mark is only an indirect vote for the president and vice-president. Our votes actually elect "electors," who assemble in December to cast their votes for the president and vice-president. The electorate does not vote directly for the president and vice-president of the United States, but instead we cast our vote for a representative who will cast the official vote for the president and vice-president. Each state has as many electors as congressional representatives plus three more for the District of Columbia for a total of 538. Therefore to win the presidency requires at least 270 electors. National news on election night reports the tally of the votes for electors.

After the election closes, electors are pledged to a candidate. The winner of the popular vote in a state receives all of the electors from that state, except for two states with a variation. Maine and Nebraska use the congressional district method, selecting one elector within each congressional district by popular vote and selecting the remaining two electors by a statewide popular vote. On Election Day, the maps on television really show the tally of electors for a candidate. The candidate that wins a majority of electors wins the presidency. The electors meet on the first Monday after the second Wednesday in December of a presidential election year. They meet in the capital of the state they represent. Their votes are transmitted to the president of the Senate, who declares the winner in front of both the House and the Senate.

There is a potential kicker. Based on how the votes go in individual states, a candidate could be elected who did not attain a majority of the votes cast, as happened in the 2000 election. Over the years, a number of Constitutional amendments have been proposed seeking to alter the Electoral College or replace it with a direct popular vote. From the National Archives website:

> *The Electoral College is a process, not a place. The founding fathers established it in the Constitution as a compromise between election of the President by a vote in Congress and election of the President by a popular vote of qualified citizens.*
>
> *The Electoral College process consists of the selection of the electors, the meeting of the electors where they vote for President and Vice President, and the counting of the electoral votes by Congress.*
>
> *The Electoral College consists of 538 electors. A majority of 270 electoral votes is required to elect the President. Your state's entitled allotment of electors equals the number of members in its Congressional delegation: one for each member in the House of Representatives plus two for your Senators ...*
>
> *Under the 23rd Amendment of the Constitution, the District of Columbia is allocated 3 electors and treated like a state for purposes of the Electoral College. For this reason, in the following discussion, the word "state" also refers to the District of Columbia.*
>
> *Each candidate running for President in your state has his or her own group of electors. The electors are generally chosen by the candidate's political party, but state laws vary on how the electors are selected and what their responsibilities are ... [Read more about the qualifications of the Electors and restrictions on who the Electors may vote for on the National Archives website: http://www.archives.gov/federal-register/electoral-college/electors.html#restrictions.]*

Whether we quickly adopt Internet e-voting or not, it's high time we change the Constitution and retire the Electoral College and codify a new election process. The Constitution created the Electoral College as a compromise so that members of Congress would not be electing the president and vice president. But with e-voting, we will have the means for electing the president and vice president by popular, direct voting. The Electoral College is an institution that has outlived its usefulness and needs to be retired. We could do away with the Electoral College before tackling e-voting with a separate amendment and allow the current election process to be revised.

We have elected presidents who did not win the popular vote. According to Fact Check, a nonpartisan, nonprofit organization whose aim is to reduce the level of confusion in U.S. politics by monitoring factual accuracy at local, state, and federal levels:

> *In 1876, Rutherford B. Hayes won the election (by a margin of one electoral vote), but he lost the popular vote by more than 250,000 ballots to Samuel J. Tilden.*
>
> *In 1888, Benjamin Harrison received 233 electoral votes to Grover Cleveland's 168, winning the presidency. But Harrison lost the popular vote by more than 90,000 votes.*
>
> *In 2000, George W. Bush was declared the winner of the general election and became the 43rd president, but he didn't win the popular vote either. Al Gore holds that distinction, garnering about 540,000 more votes than Bush. However, Bush won the electoral vote, 271 to 266.*

Among reasons, however, to retain the Electoral College would be to lessen the chance for an outcome where there is no clear winner of the office of president on election night. Richard A. Posner posits several reasons for retaining the Electoral College at Slate.com. The possibility of runoff elections stands as the most potentially troubling one:

*The Electoral College avoids the problem of elections in which no candidate receives a majority of the votes cast. For example, Nixon in 1968 and Clinton in 1992 both had only a 43 percent plurality of the popular votes, while winning a majority in the Electoral College (301 and 370 electoral votes, respectively). There is pressure for runoff elections when no candidate wins a majority of the votes cast; that pressure, which would greatly complicate the presidential election process, is reduced by the Electoral College, which invariably produces a clear winner.*

The Electoral College was created to solve the problems of the eighteenth century. Now, it hinders the full potential of a modern democracy. When relying on the Electoral College if we have a candidate who fails to win a popular majority but still wins the most votes, that person becomes the president. Bill Clinton won with 43 percent of the popular vote in 1992 but achieved a majority in the Electoral College. A National Constitutional Convention would be tasked with looking at all the options for replacing the Electoral College to come up with the best solution. But with Internet e-voting, we could easily handle runoff elections if we decide that any president must win by a majority of the popular vote. Voters would have to vote again—that's all. What's so terrible about that? Other nations handle runoff elections successfully. As a democracy, we are mature enough to handle a runoff election. If a runoff election was designed to conduct the runoff between the two highest vote getters, then a third-party candidate (and others) could not participate in the final runoff election. It's that simple. Some voters would have to make a different choice. It is really a fairer way to handle the desires of the voters.

## Reasons to Retire the Electoral College

First, the Electoral College allows the election of a candidate who could win the nation's highest office with less than a majority of votes. A president could be elected and take office if, as in 1888, one candidate's popular support was heavily concentrated in a few states while the other candidate maintained a slim popular lead in enough states to win the needed majority of the Electoral College. With the technological tools and polling sophistication available to the two major parties, a strategy to elect a candidate could be crafted in a way to focus on the Electoral College votes. As our nation gets larger and larger, the risk of the election for president could be determined by fewer and fewer voters in key states.

Second, an elector could choose to cast their vote for someone other than the candidate they were selected to represent. This occurred only once in recent times, when an elector for West Virginia cast his vote for Lloyd Bentsen for president and Michael Dukakis for vice-president as a protest. There was no impact since the Electoral College vote for Ronald Reagan was overwhelming. But it indicates a weak point, a potential flaw, in the system.

Third, the Electoral College results have not always reflected the popular vote. Because smaller and rural states have more representatives per voter, they also get more electors. Using facts from the 1988 election again, we find that the combined voting age population (3,119,000) of the seven least populous jurisdictions of Alaska, Delaware, the District of Columbia, North Dakota, South Dakota, Vermont, and Wyoming carried the same voting strength in the Electoral College (twenty-one electoral votes) as the 9,614,000 persons of voting age in the State of Florida. Therefore, each Floridian's vote carried about one-third the weight of a potential vote in the other states listed. The Electoral College violates or at least skews the core concept of one person, one vote.

Adding each state's senators into the Electoral College mix means that smaller states have more electoral votes proportionally than larger states. We'll discuss this more in a later chapter, but for now, this is an argument to either do away with the Electoral College or to restrict the size of the Electoral College to the number of representatives a state has been allocated. Generally, it is fair to say that the Electoral College just doesn't fit the makeup of the electorate.

## Reasons to Retain the Electoral College

First, acknowledging the strong regional interests and loyalties that have played so great a role in American history, proponents argue that the Electoral College system contributes to the cohesiveness of the country by requiring a distribution of popular support to be elected president; without such a mechanism, the president could be selected either through the domination of one populous region over others or through the domination of large metropolitan areas over rural ones. Indeed, it is principally because of the Electoral College that presidential nominees are inclined to select vice presidential running mates from a region other than their own. As things stand now, no one region contains the absolute majority of electoral votes (270) required to elect a president. Thus, there is an incentive for presidential candidates to pull together coalitions of states and regions rather than to exacerbate regional differences.

Second, voters from minority or special interests groups can enhance the value of getting out the vote because the Electoral College actually enhances the status of minority groups. Voters of even small minorities in a state may make the difference between winning all of that state's electoral votes or none of that state's electoral votes. And since ethnic minority groups in the United States happen to concentrate in those states with the most electoral votes, they assume an importance to presidential candidates out of proportion to their number. The same concept could apply to other special interest groups, such as labor unions, farmers, environmentalists, and so forth. Changing to a direct election of the president could therefore actually damage minority interests, since their votes would be overwhelmed by a national popular majority.

Third, utilizing the Electoral College maintains and enhances our two-party system. Major parties have every incentive to absorb minor party movements in their continual attempt to win popular majorities in the states. In this process of assimilation, third-party movements are obliged to compromise their more radical views if they hope to attain any of their more generally acceptable objectives. Thus we end up with two large, pragmatic political parties rather than dozens of smaller political parties catering to divergent and sometimes extremist views. In other words, such a system forces political coalitions to occur within the political parties rather than within the government.

## The Very Thought of Change is Difficult

The Electoral College was established through a series of deliberations and compromises when the nation formed. It was impractical to have Congress choose a president since it would be too divisive and destructive within that body. Allowing state legislatures to elect the president was rejected out of fear that federal authority could be eroded and the president swayed by larger states. Finally, direct election was rejected not because voters were considered incapable but because they would only know those candidates nearest to them. There were no national campaigns at that time. As a result, the original National Constitutional Convention proposed the Electoral College.

If we could all agree that present circumstances and technology no longer require continuing the Electoral College, several difficulties remain. First is that doing away with the Electoral College requires an amendment to the Constitution—a difficult undertaking under any circumstances. Second, change is difficult to absorb and accept. We are used to the excitement of network television calling a state and its electoral votes for a candidate as we watch the map turn red or blue. Third, we don't do well changing deeply held beliefs. A change such as this requires a campaign that changes both hearts and minds.

Persons who leave their religion or church don't always pick up another church or belief system. It's easier to just walk away from a belief. Look at scientific debates over the years, even when evidence is present. Businesses don't do well with change either. Most often someone determines what changes will take place and that's the end of it. We can neither abandon nor walk away from electing a president and vice-president. We will have to imagine millions of votes marked and tallied that will provide a number that indicates which party won an election. Maybe the solution is not to allow networks to broadcast any election results until the last ballots are cast.

If we allow e-voting, then we will not be able to release tallies until all the voting windows close. The networks will use polls as a substitute for how an election has progressed. The disclosure of polling results will have to be prohibited. But we are not a citizenry used to waiting. We want elections to look like major league sports events with scores and the lead shifting from one to another. Friends, that's no way to run a country. In former times, election results took days and weeks to tally. We can figure out how to delay the gratification of outcomes a little while.

## Summary

E-voting and the elimination of the Electoral College will require amendments to the Constitution. If the nation calls a National Constitutional Convention, each one could be treated separately so that any amendments would go to the state legislatures separately. They do not have to be linked.

It is always possible that a third-party candidate could win enough votes to become one of the two run-off candidates. This could potentially change the dynamics of presidential elections. It could give a new third party a chance it would not get under the current circumstances. One might argue that there is nothing stopping a third party from coming into existence, but by allowing only direct election of the president and vice-president, a third party has a better chance to gather support year after year. If we retired the Electoral College and created other reforms around presidential elections and fundraising, we might revitalize the prospects of different kinds of presidential candidates beyond what we get now.

Every day we, as a nation, get the opportunity to do things differently if only we want to. Change is a hallmark of a dynamic, energetic society. We must not enslave our future to the past. We at least owe it to each other to examine every two to three hundred years if what we're doing is still the best method. When we went off to school, we did not know which subject would be our best one until we studied a subject. Life for nations can also be an exciting adventure. We can do better. We don't have to retire the Electoral College, but we need to know if it's still the best method we have for electing the best person to the most important job in the world.

# CHAPTER 7

## We Are Responsible for Our Nation

• • •

*Sometimes it falls upon a generation to be great.*
*You can be that great generation. Let your greatness*
*blossom.*

—Nelson Mandela

Democracies are like volunteer organizations that are highly dependent on the labor, concern, ideas, and energy of those who have experienced injustice or loss coupled with a myriad of idealists and dreamers. Historically, when democracies become overly reliant on paid bureaucracies and consultants, they become less responsive to the will of the people. In the cases of governments based on a monarch or dictator, such bureaucracies served at the privilege of the monarch, rather than the people. If we look at fledgling democracies in Africa, for example, we can see how little it takes to make democracy vanish. We must be ever vigilant.

One has only to look at the hundreds of thousands of people who make their living inside the Beltway or connected to Washington, D.C. politics to realize that many of the people who make decisions about the future of America are not elected through a democratic process. Furthermore, many of the people we do legally elect are unduly influenced by such people.

There is a strong argument to be made that we as a nation, with millions of participants (or non-participants) in our democracy, are not taking the responsibility that we should for the future of the country and the overall health of our democratic system of governance. We are in fact responsible for our nation, and if we don't like how business is being conducted inside the Beltway, we are obligated and empowered to do something about it.

Why aren't Americans taking more responsibility for where we are as a nation? There are many possible answers to this question, and many of them have some degree of truth to them.

Some suggested explanations include:

- Why should I care? One vote doesn't make a difference anyway...
- I'm sick of partisanship. Until the parties can get their acts together, I'm not getting involved.
- My work demands more and more of me (and labor statistics bear this out). I don't have time to be a more active citizen.
- I don't feel connected to people. (The twenty-first century has seen the breakdown of traditional social groups.)
- Everything is becoming too big.
- I have to move for my job. I don't have an opportunity to become vested in community activities or elections.
- My preferences don't matter; my voice doesn't matter. (Actually, the marketing folks at Pepsi and other corporations do care about your preferences, and know all about them—consumer voices do matter to them!)

The challenge is to bring our democracy back into balance so that the average voter feels like they do make a difference and have more opportunity for input. To do that will require what corporations refer to as disruptive technology, or change that will be uncomfortable. In our case, amendments to the Constitution historically act as disruptive technologies. Corporations also rely on disruptive technology to expand markets and introduce new products and ideas. As we've suggested earlier in this book, bringing about innovation will require a series of constitutional amendments.

## We Can No Longer Wait on Our Leaders to Act

There is no end of books, articles, broadcasts, and speeches prompting readers to contact their elected representatives and become more active in the political process. The admonition to the reader or the audience by so many writers and commentators is an imperfect call to become more engaged politically. We have Facebook and

Twitter where we can talk with each other about these things. But the only step that might currently achieve any action between elections requires us to send a letter or make a phone call to our congressional representatives or senators. We will forever be pushing on a string using this method. The nation wants more results than it sees from its government. It is now time to bring about some direct, popular democracy in the United States. We presume if you're reading this you are well aware of the challenges facing our nation. No matter a person's political preferences, there is nowhere to take suggested solutions except to the halls of Congress. It's actually our sacred responsibility to do that.

Here we define a set of possible solutions for current and future challenges that will come our way. We suggest that the twentieth century was the zenith of the great-leader democracy when nations were led by presidents and prime ministers who proposed a vision, inspired citizens, and made conditions better for the majority of us. But the twenty-first century will see the rise of the great citizen-led democracy because we have the means and the will to do it. We want to pick up where Adams and Jefferson left off and continue to revise the way we govern ourselves by including the tools available in the twenty-first century. We want to elevate our ideas into a framework that allows action. This is not new either. George Burns joked, "Too bad that all the people that know how to run the country are busy driving taxicabs and cutting hair." We share one common heritage and now we need to redirect our thoughts and ideas into a common vision. Great leaders are few and far between, but every day, millions of capable people put their feet on the floor and should be devoting a portion of their vision and energy to citizenship opportunities during the year to revitalize our nation for themselves and their children and their children's children out to the Seventh Generation.

Our Constitution was not meant to be replaced but to be amended. Sometimes we live in apartments until we save enough for a house. Once a family starts to grow, then a move to a larger house may be required. But many times, once we find our home, we add on to it or remodel it rather than continue to move. Our citizen family has grown and grown and will continue to grow. Voters are the head of the family, and it is our responsibility to remodel where we live. We inherited a grand eighteenth-century house on a hill, and we wish to continue to live in it. But it needs its wiring replaced and needs more rooms and other improvements. We are taking something that is grand and now we will together make it grander. We will let more light in.

## Belief and Encouragement

To make the significant and difficult changes that this book espouses, it will take a belief by everyone that change can be accomplished successfully, that we will create a fairer government, and that by insisting on having more input into governance, we will make our nation more consistently optimistic and confident. Belief is a partner with mutual responsibility.

We must become a nation of encouragers. Those left out or left behind will see a way to rejoin the conversation and be heard if we complete our remodeling. We must stop the bickering that splits us apart and keeps us apart. We need new ways to talk to each other about problems. The word *they* can no longer be the word that starts political discussions about change. We will add new words to our nation's vocabulary. The first one is *us*.

In 1822, William Tudor proposed the idea of a monument to commemorate the start of the American Revolution. Around 1818, a method of drilling holes in granite and splitting it to make blocks of stone started the great "Stone Age" of New England architecture. Solomon Willard, who only had a grade school education, was selected to construct the monument out of granite. In 1825, the Bunker Hill Monument Association purchased a granite quarry in Quincy. Willard not only constructed the monument but also invented nearly every piece of equipment later used in the granite industry. The population of Massachusetts in 1825 was around 550,000. Look at this example of American ingenuity from the population of an entire state that today equals a small city. Solomon Willard applied his common sense to a difficult undertaking. Every generation must go to places no one has been before.

We do not lack talent—we lack opportunity. Can we not apply our talents to ideas the same way Solomon Willard applied his ingenuity to harvesting granite? Can we not create, like Willard, the same kind of new equipment used to quarry and lift granite? We need to quarry and lift ideas of the mind to construct additions to the Constitution. We live in a nation crowded with genius going to waste. Citizen voters need new opportunities to apply the talents they inherited. Congress is a primary place where that opportunity can originate. But that opportunity also rests on the shoulders of voters. How are our desires different from Americans in 1825? We have cars and smart phones, but our desire for safety, education, and opportunity have not changed that much except perhaps we want more than they expected, and we need tools for the new world.

Even during the Civil War, our nation continued to construct the dome of the capitol. Leaders at that time were wise and understood that even a terrible war can't stop democracy from moving forward. We're adding another dome onto the Constitution to expand democracy by keeping what we have and adding to it. By doing this, we will lead the way again for all nations to show where democracy is headed and what it can achieve by uniting our republic with e-democracy, technology, and our Constitution in a new way. This will also keep democracy fresh and renewed.

## Preconditions for Change

We must first accept responsibility for the world we live in and the one we will leave behind when we are gone. No more fundamental requirement exists if you have enjoyed even one day in this great nation.

> *The century upon which we have just entered must inevitably be one of tremendous triumph or of tremendous failure for the whole human race, because, to an infinitely greater extent than ever before, humanity is knit together in all its parts, for weal or woe.*
>
> – President Theodore Roosevelt while vice-president at the Pan-American Exposition, 1901

We believe that democracy itself is endangered as the middle class declines, as special interest groups get stronger, and as the word "compromise" has been banned from consideration in every deliberation between parties. The last impactful Constitutional amendment passed nearly four decades ago, and the most recent amendment took 202 years to ratify and only affected members of Congress. We must look to ourselves (citizen leaders) to establish a vision for the long-term course that politics and legislation must take. You can find the new leader of this fine country by looking into a mirror hanging in your home!

Amendments are the evolution of democracy, but these kinds of changes share some of the fundamental conditions that led to the great revolutions. Much of what follows is pulled from *Anatomy of Revolution* by Crane Brinton. One of the fundamental ideas he expressed was that revolutions occur not when things are really bad but when conditions improved and then went back into decline. The 1980s and 1990s could be described as "good times" running up to 2007 to 2008 when the financial crisis occurred. Many people in the middle class have been in economic decline since then, and those below the middle class have not experienced any lift in a long, long time. At this time, the prognosis remains uncertain, but there is a growing sense that something needs to change.

France before the revolution of 1789 may have some similarities with our situation today. France, as an economy, was financially sound in 1789. But the government was near bankruptcy after a series of wars from 1740 to 1783. The aristocracy vetoed attempts to reform tax policy. The middle class resented their lack of political power. Many aristocrats fought to retain their class privileges, particularly their monopoly of high offices (military, church, and, to a lesser extent, bureaucracy), blocking the rise of men of ability from the lower and middle classes. Simply put, inequality was rising then. Fast-forward to today to our own nation and we can feel discontent rising within many groups. The shooting of Michael Brown in Ferguson, Missouri, in 2014 and the death of Freddie Gray in police custody in Baltimore on April 19, 2015 sparked demonstrations against police behavior and procedures in both localities. The discontent among middle-class Republicans in 2016 fueled the candidacy of Donald Trump. On the other end of the spectrum, many younger voters are supporting the candidacy of Bernie Sanders for president. Any radical change begins on the fringe and can spread to the center. Events are priming the pump for major change in the way we govern ourselves.

Signs of discontent can be found in many areas in our country.

Unions feel they are being pushed out while state legislators feel that unions raise costs for industry unnecessarily. Parents feel that their children do not get the kind of education for the taxes they paid. The middle class feels trapped. The upper classes feel that they are paying more than their share and supporting too many "deadbeats." But we can restore prosperity and optimism to all if our sense of joint purpose allows us to update the way we govern ourselves.

## The Only Direction Is Forward

Governance is a complex undertaking. Laws and rules must be put in place yet remain flexible or revoked quickly if they prove ineffective. We need to apply systems thinking to come up with solutions. The immigration problem is not just about the borders. It's about health care, education, and employment, too. We cannot solve just one problem without looking at all the impacts that go along with it. By comparison, the CEO of General Motors has an easier job than Congress. A redesign of our system will be the first step. In what follows, we will lay out a constitutional framework that will enable the renewal of our governance.

We are, as we've said, a nation filled with talent. We need to harness ideas from every university, corporation, and think tank. Currently, every solution we have come across relies upon that solution being adopted by Congress, the very group that often impedes reform. Voters will have to elect legislators at every level who will promise to call a constitutional convention so that the appropriate parts of the Constitution can be changed.

Our history is filled with examples of collectively taking responsibility. Education is a prime example. Our university and college system began with a few localized efforts, often focused through the church and on the clergy, but today represents a network of thousands of schools that provide two- and four-year degrees as well as countless certifications. Many of the schools remain not for profit and exist primarily to promote the benefits of a practical and theoretical educational experience. Likewise, the K12 educational reform movement of the antebellum era culminated after the Civil War in an inclusive public school system, which now denies no child access to a "free and appropriate public education."

Our educational system did not evolve by accident, and it often evolved with the help of a democratically driven national government in collaboration with states. It served a national purpose, improved the economic situation of everyone, and was seen as part of a healthy democracy. When it became apparent to leaders like John Dewey that education should be a national priority, voters elected representatives who promoted education. We collectively took responsibility for a need that we shared.

Another example comes from transportation and infrastructure. Although the interstate road system was developed in the 1950s as a direct effort at national security (the Cold War), in fact it quickly grew into a commercial lifeline that has spawned enormous economic growth and national benefit. This extensive road network is not something that individual states could have coordinated or funded in ways that the federal government was able to. This road system has actually contributed to the health of our democratic way of life, which embraces freedom of movement and economic choice. People are free to live where they want to and, in many cases, work where they want to as well. We collectively took responsibility for a national initiative to ensure mobility and opportunity (and at the same time to help our national security).

There are many other examples of Americans collectively taking responsibility for the health of their country and their democracy. We currently live in a time, however, where there are real questions about the health of our democracy and the extent to which we are still taking mutual responsibility. The immigration challenges in Texas, for example, may not seem that important to the city dwellers in Detroit (who have their own set of problems to deal with), but the Fourth Branch is arguing that we all have responsibility for both situations, collectively, and that a healthy democracy can effectively deal with them.

We must, once again as we've done before, take constitutional responsibility for where we are and for how we can promote a healthy, responsive democracy to deal with the challenges of our time. The Fourth Branch offers both hope and solutions, within our constitutional framework. We may, if we do it right, foster a democracy that can be better prepared for the uncertain future.

# CHAPTER 8

## Power Channels

• • •

*The only place success comes before work is in the dictionary.*

—Vince Lombardi

We must turn our attention to defining the location of power and a path to it. Just as scientists conduct experiments, we must also set up experiments or methodologies to determine what power we need to accumulate in order to bring change—not more than we need but enough to change the course, similar to the way engineers divert a river from its current path when they need to build a dam across a river. To bring about changes to the degree put forth in these pages through amendments to the Constitution will require the unification of many different political ideologies. Changes to the Constitution can be accomplished by the passage of amendments by two-thirds majority from both Houses of Congress or by two-thirds of state legislatures voting to call a National Constitutional Convention. Either way still requires ratification of proposed changes by three-fourths of state legislatures. Either method will be a difficult but necessary approach since we no longer believe that change can come about without modifying the framework of the Constitution.

We want to introduce the term *power channels*—ways to assess how direct power and influence work in groups. Power channels can only be built over time. For example, the power of the president of the United States comes from the strength of the nation supporting the office and the history of the office and the prestige of the people of those who have held the office. Most offices and positions come with a degree of power. The concept of power channels examines how threads of power, both individual and in groups, can be combined to become circular definition. Instead, we will discuss power channels in terms of individual voters and the Constitution.

> *I am not interested in power for power's sake, but I'm interested in power that is moral, that is right and that is good.*
>
> —Martin Luther King, Jr.

In January of 2011, a wide swath of Egyptian society, determined to bring down the autocratic Mubarak regime, showed the world a new method to usher in governmental reform. The tools of social media, such as Twitter and Facebook, coalesced in a way that allowed disaffected people to unite to remove an autocratic presidency and lay the groundwork for an environment for democracy. What previously had been messages focused on raising general awareness suddenly became focused and compounded, growing strong enough to challenge Mubarak's authority. Enough people took action by reaching out to others and taking to the streets to cause the world to take notice. Social media coupled with a single purpose (to bring down Mubarak) created a power channel where none had existed before. Sustained demonstrations created a level of intensity and interest to tip the scales in favor of the demonstrators. The goal was to overthrow Mubarak, and the means were social media tools. In that moment, everyone on the planet received an Egyptian passport! Social media made us citizens of a virtual nation. Websites, Twitter feeds, Facebook, and cell phones united in a single purpose, becoming the twenty-first century's version of a battering ram that would shatter the gates protecting special interests and a self-serving dictator. A large number of people channeled their desires and beliefs into a single objective.

American history has numerous examples of such potent forces where power channels come together. The Civil Rights Movement is the most prominent example. The Civil Rights power channel consisted of a dynamic leader, Rev. Martin Luther King Jr., Southern African-American churches, student groups, and many other sympathizers. The Civil Rights power channel formed from all the smaller tributary power channels the way a river gathers waters so in the end the primary power channel is a raging torrent that nothing can stand in the way of. The Civil Rights Act of 1964 marked a significant milestone. It remains to this day a channel that achieves goals when enough others band with it. The shooting on June 17, 2015 at the Emanuel A.M.E. Church in Charleston, South Carolina, created a spontaneous power channel that forced the removal of some of the last vestiges of the Confederate flag.

Change in the twenty-first century requires an astounding majority to unite to create a power channel capable of overcoming existing power structures, which become intransigent simply because they are in place. The work of each new generation, each infant idea, is difficult because something else must be moved or removed to make way for it.

Creating the Constitution was difficult for the founders of this nation. But they only needed to replace the Articles of Confederation, created solely to conduct the war for our independence. The Articles of Confederation were not particularly strong to begin with. Nevertheless, it took considerable effort by our Founding Fathers to create a constitution when no sense of a nation existed yet and then modify the proposed constitution through compromise to get it ratified.

Every person owns their small power channel and an influence channel. These channels are the degree to which an individual can impact the world around us, immediate or long term. These channels can be operational, dormant, or constrained, weak or strong, and short or long. Channels can end or have very long tails like comets. For example, the writings of Martin Luther King Jr. make his power and influence channel operational, strong, and long. When he was able to stand before an audience or march in the streets, he merged his influence channels leading others to action with him and rallying the support of other groups such as clergy to join with his objectives. The clergy then utilized their ability to influence others to band with the Civil Rights power channel, thereby increasing the power and influence of the Civil Rights Movement more and more. Students and whites in the New Left also joined their power channels to the Civil Rights channel. We will use power channel as the term that denotes both power and influence since they are so closely bound.

The plainest definition of *power* is "the ability or capacity to perform or act effectively." *Influence* on the other hand is "the capacity or power of persons or things to be a compelling force on or produce effects on the actions, behavior, opinions, etc., of others."

Influence begins as a thought in the brain and evolves into a desire to communicate that thought. The act of communicating the thought is an attempt to influence or persuade. An idea communicated to someone else, either as an individual communication or to a mass audience, creates the on-ramp to power. We can think of many examples of when a person with real power can compel action, such as a general issuing orders to an army. Sometimes, depending on circumstances, that person may instead choose to use influence instead. The nature of the goal determines if a power channel uses influence only, power only, or a combination of the two. The boundary between influence and power cannot be explicitly defined. When someone hears a message and believes that message, then we suggest a power channel is born.

Demonstrations in the streets of Cairo during the Arab Spring of 2011 showed the existence of a power channel even though no direct means was available to cause Mubarak to resign. The intent was to marshal enough pressure for him to relinquish his power voluntarily. When the demonstrators would not obey commands to clear Tahrir Square, what started as protests to influence the government of Mubarak became a full-fledged power channel because the refusal of the crowd to disburse was a real sign of the movement's power. Power channels, like flood waters, are additive, and when combined can quickly change the outcome of a situation. Once Mubarak resigned, there was no need to continue demonstrations and therefore the influence and power dissipated since the objective was achieved. Subsequent events demonstrated that the power channel did not attain enough power to prevent the military from taking over. Similarly, a power channel terminates when there is no more capacity or interest in acting effectively. Today, Mubarak has no power; his power channel ended as well.

Interestingly, Mubarak understood power channels. After Anwar Sadat was assassinated, Mubarak succeeded him. Mubarak, who was slightly wounded during the attack on Sadat, reorganized the military in such a way as to prevent officers from forming ties with each other, even informal ties. Mubarak was well aware of the potential power of the military to combine individual power channels with a larger channel. Robert Springborg, an expert on the Egyptian military, said that direct email communications among officers was prohibited under Mubarak. This is an example of constraining the power channel of others. Mubarak prevented the use of influence that could lead to shifting currents of power.

Power and influence channels are multi-dimensional. Sometimes it is an on/off switch, such as the power channel of an emergency room surgeon who stops the immediate bleeding of an injured patient and then hands the patient over to another doctor for more specialized surgery. Each heath care entity has a high degree of power over various stages of the patient's recovery. Teachers and religious leaders can influence others as well, but sometimes have limited direct power and often create more subtle channels that aren't as visible. Family physicians, to give another example, do not have the direct power to force their patients to follow a healthier diet, but they try to influence their patients nonetheless through education and other less direct channels.

Power channels work both directly and indirectly. A powerful speech can have an immediate influence. If the audience recalls the speech for years afterwards, like the speeches of Peggy Noonan that Ronald Reagan delivered with such presence, then the influence of the speech has a long "tail." A power channel usually has a more defined boundary than an influence channel. For example, governors of states have the most power within their own states, obviously. They may have influence outside of their state when attending a National Governors Association meeting or when interviewed on television, but power basically stops at the border of a state. But the actions of a governor in one state can influence the actions of other governors or other states. Leaders of nations have power and influence beyond their borders based on their nation's economic, military, or cultural components. Power and influence channels are dynamic and multidimensional. They represent a person's touch points with their environment and other power channels. The more power and influence an individual has, the more his/her channels are likely to become and remain more complex, wider, and deeper.

Power channels, however, are fragmented, like the delta at the end of the river. For example, between elections the electorate can only operate within its influence channel, which is primarily limited to phone calls, letters, and emails to elected officials. Although the electorate has the power to change the person in an official office through voting, its power channel is really only operational during the election cycle of a representative, for example. Additionally, a single voter's power is limited to the border of the district they live in.

The election of the president is not a direct vote since technically the electorate votes for electors who meet to actually select the president of the United States.

In the summer of 2011, voters in Wisconsin used the power of recall to force special elections in the Senate, where many voters opposed the perceived attacks on labor rights, local democracy, public education, and basic services. Only nineteen states even allow use of the recall ballot. This kind of power channel requires a minimum number of signatures before it can be set into motion. If you graph power channels, you will see spikes when they can achieve goals, similar to how rivers can be charted for seasonal flow. Power channels are difficult to sustain for individuals, unless you happen to be an elected official or a chief executive officer or someone who has been handed a larger power channel by appointment.

The electorate's power is very weak and constrained compared to its potential influence. Voting for someone is the electorate's attempt to influence the outcome of laws. We live in a nation of laws, but only a few make those laws directly. The only way voters achieve a direct say in the passage of a law is when a potential law has gone through the petition process and appears on the ballot. These are rare events (some would say "thankfully"). The ability of voters to exercise either power or influence is sporadic due to the nature of election cycles and the current format of power channels. Voters do not have continuous power and few opportunities to interject their will outside of the election cycle.

Not only are power and influence channels fragmentary by nature, they become more fragmentary in situations where everyone believes that their way is the true standard that the entire population should follow. In America, we have celebrated rugged individualism, but democracy may in fact be better served by collective responsibility. The proliferation of social media and specialized media outlets demonstrates that there are literally millions of people with similar beliefs on any given topic. We don't have to go alone. In such a fertile environment, a movement or belief system can proliferate or strengthen if power channels combine.

There are strong forces in our current two-party system that often works against combining power channels. In some situations, power channels are seemingly diverted intentionally, just to slow down progress. One position or set of beliefs can immediately breed opposing positions. This is not a new problem. Strong opinions and misguided beliefs, which sometimes come about as a reaction to another constructive idea, have been harnessed for all sorts of purposes throughout history, not all of them positive. Beneficial laws such as child labor laws came about as a response to reports of abuse by tabloids and investigators, who influenced popular opinion to the point that change occurred in the halls of power. A few repugnant ideas have become law as well, such as the passage of the poll tax to stymie voter rights in Southern states, a reaction against the Thirteenth Amendment. The new ingredient in our time is the rapidity with which any idea or belief can attain a level of credence among a large number of people, even in an irrational counter reaction. Ideas can now be heated quickly in the microwave of today's media—both traditional and social. New social media enables ideas to jump from one individual's channel to another's, and in the process combine smaller channels into a significant and formidable influence. Change can occur quickly. Generally, however, influence remains fragmentary, and it is up to individuals to consciously decide to combine their channels.

Very few individuals operate purely at the power channel level most of the time. In democratic societies, the head of government also has to utilize the exercise of influence to achieve goals by other means. An executive order signed by the president of the United States is an example of power. If the president hammers out a bipartisan agreement on an issue, then the influence of the office is manifest. Both actions involve power channels. In autocratic or dictatorial governments, the leader may be able to exercise more power than influence. Change can occur faster under circumstances where many individuals have a high awareness of their own power channels.

An individual's power channel varies greatly, however, based on many other variables such as culture, geography, and economic factors. Often in the United States, we believe that economic factors alone are the primary basis for someone's power channel, but it is only one of several variables. There are also examples of power and influence channels created by people such as Mother Teresa, Sigmund Freud, Mahatma Gandhi, Theodore Roosevelt, John Muir, and Clara Barton, whose power or influence continue to operate to some degree beyond their lifetimes. For example, Theodore Roosevelt as president issued executive orders setting aside areas to serve as national wildlife preserves. John Muir used influence to get Yosemite

National Park established. He also founded the Sierra Club, whose power and influence can be brought to bear on issues today, thereby maintaining a power channel that he created. Clara Barton founded the American Red Cross on May 21, 1881, thereby establishing an organization whose power is most often demonstrated during times of disaster or hardship. Even when a leader founds and then later leaves an organization, to a significant extent his or her power continues, as long as the organization continues to support the original mission.

In education, teachers often work tirelessly to educate our young citizens, and yet they often don't know the final outcome of the students' journeys. Years later, a student might come back and say thank you for how much that teacher meant to them. The power channel that teacher created was significant, but not evident. Many power channels operate this way. Teachers even have faith they are making a difference, even when they don't receive constant feedback. Voters must have a similar faith.

People in more obvious positions of power can make significant changes for good or evil. There are plenty of examples of powerful, cruel tyrants. Democracy, dating back to ancient Greece, is a story of citizens and organizations that use power channels to influence or to prod those in power to create the outcomes the voters desire.

A power channel is the sum of all the levers at the disposal of an individual to affect outcomes based on their own beliefs and priorities. I push my trash bin to the curb once a week. This action is dictated by the way trash disposal operates in my suburban neighborhood. I am dependent on my job for the funds to pay a company to pick up the refuse while both the trash company and I depend on the municipal authority to maintain and preserve the resource that will allow us to deposit trash in a landfill (and maintain the roads the truck drives on). If I wish to change the way we dispose of trash and garbage, then I will have to join my influence channel to the influence channels of others and ultimately connect to the power channel of municipal supervisors in order to create a change. So if the desired outcome was to create a less wasteful disposal system, then it would require a large effort of many people to move through the influence process to apply sufficient pressure that supervisors would act to implement any change.

Because Americans have been trained for so long to be rugged individuals, we sometimes tend to shout louder on our own rather than try to recruit others to speak with us. Unfortunately, many current power channels, or authorities, find it easy to ignore the lone wolf or the squeaky wheel. When we join together, officials must take note.

When one power or influence channel joins another power channel, this is a *connection point*. Change comes from the confluence of connection points that increase the chances of change actually occurring because of the accumulation of channels. Although other factors, such as the economic status and education of a family, affect the dimensions of any individual's power channel, those factors do not negate the potential for any power channel to add to a movement. Influence is the engine that drives the ability to impact power channels and thereby create new outcomes and directions. Leadership is the captain in the wheelhouse directing the power of others, but it should always stem from the combination of voter power channels.

## Summary

So much political and economic infrastructure has become layered within our increasingly complex system that to make meaningful changes requires much more significant, sustained effort. This may be why so many individual voters feel like they might not be able to make a difference. We still have "one person equals one vote," and we don't realize in many cases that our power channel is still intact, and waiting to be fully utilized when combined with others. While there are many great things about our country that still work well, there is also a significant level of dissatisfaction with many of our democratic processes.

It won't require as much effort as many think to set up prototypes to test potential changes. If the changes work well, then building support for the changes will not be as daunting. Voters will more energetically combine their power channels. For example, a prototype of Internet e-voting could be created and tested before going to a new voting system. It would still require the creation of a significant movement (a power channel) to even get this much set up. Making the effort to change the Constitution to implement e-voting permanently may be the best approach (and again utilizes another major power channel). We must come together to decide these things first.

To call a constitutional convention will require almost everyone to focus on the one task of assembling the required congressional or state legislature votes to initiate the process. Almost every citizen-based organization would need to get behind it, along with enough voters to convince either Congress or a super-majority of statehouses to call a convention. But if this is what we the voters want, no one can stop us. Calling a constitutional convention is a tool the founders gave us very intentionally. Delegates to the convention would have to propose the wording of amendments, which would then go the state legislatures for them to ratify.

It requires broad support for an idea using every means available to convince Congress to call a constitutional convention. It will necessarily transcend party, political ideologies, and regionalism. The degree of cooperation required is not unprecedented, but it is unusual in a population of our size.

To even talk about the specifics of design and implementation will require large-scale cooperation among a very diverse population swayed by a number of beliefs and crosscurrents. But that is the way the United States historically achieved its greatness. When we squabble, we weaken ourselves. When we talk and have a dialogue together, we grow stronger. We may be accustomed to the way things work even when we don't like them, but we should never give in to the notion that they can't be changed. The effort to get consensus is not beyond our reach. If enough of us join our hands, our minds, and our hearts for longer than twenty minutes, we have no idea how far we can go. Someone once said, "Shoot for the stars and maybe you'll hit the treetops!" Our nation has already proven we have the talent to go far above the treetops. We need to look at taking our political structures to the next level; it will take a unified commitment.

# CHAPTER 9

## Amendments—The Maternity Ward of the Constitution

• • •

*Let us not seek the Republican answer or the
Democratic answer, but the right answer. Let us not
seek to fix the blame for the past. Let us accept our
own responsibility for the future.*

—John F. Kennedy

Whether we were born in this country or came to it, when we arrived all the institutions already existed, each one with a long history and established by ancestors who lived in a very different era. We probably spent very little time pondering if we had the best government, best roads, best schools, and best laws. All the major structures were already set; a current leadership was in place. We spend most of our lives fitting into the slots already made readily available to us in society.

But when change is necessary or beneficial, it means by definition modifying the structures. Our founders in one sense worked from scratch, and sometimes people suggest that they had an easy setup. From another perspective, they had to look beyond the structures that we had from King George and Great Britain and literally break free into a new way of thinking. Change has never been easy, even when a rebellion against a colonial power resulted in the opportunity to make a new nation. Change, by its nature, requires a level of commitment and a willingness to move out of the old tracks and envision new ways.

The amazing aspect about change from an American point of view is that our founders anticipated the need for change, and they even designed and built our government to allow for it. They also understood the challenges that come with potential change, and they left us many inspiring examples of how to overcome inertia and fear. It is remarkable that we have not had a National Constitutional Convention since 1780s, and yet it is a tool the founders clearly intended for us to use.

One way to change things is to run for office. Another is to start a movement that will result in a change to the law. Sometimes those methods have worked well enough. We have only occasionally used the biggest tool in our constitutional toolbox, the amendment process, to modify the way we govern ourselves and envision our future.

We argue that there has not been an amendment to the Constitution since the 1960s. The Twenty-sixth Amendment, ratified in 1971, was an outgrowth of the Vietnam War. We drafted eighteen-year-olds to fight and die for their country but they could not vote in elections. This amendment lowered the voting age to eighteen. The Twenty-seventh Amendment, passed in 1992, was proposed at the start of the republic, over two hundred years ago. It simply states that any raise Congress votes for itself cannot take effect until after the next election of legislators. The amendment languished for over two hundred years before receiving enough votes in statehouses to be ratified and become part of the Constitution. This amendment did not impact anyone directly outside of Washington, D.C.

Presently, constitutional change is at a full stop. That's not because people haven't tried. There have literally been thousands of amendments proposed at lower levels, and none of them have reached the level of serious consideration at the national congressional level, with perhaps the exception of the currently unratified Equal Rights Amendment (ERA). In essence, there has been a lot of wind in the sails of constitutional amendments, but the ship has gone in circles.

There were problems to be sure during all periods of our history. Beginning in the 1950s, we protested the lack of civil rights. In the sixties, we protested our involvement in the Vietnam War and marched to end the war. We also had movements to eradicate poverty and raise women's rights issues. But we never questioned that we had the best framework of governance of any nation. To achieve progress, we wrote to legislators, wrote letters to the editors of papers, and marched in the streets. There was tremendous progress in many areas and sometimes general satisfaction with the way our presidents, governors, and legislators ran the nation. But most of the progress we look back on came from laws, executive orders, and Supreme Court rulings. We did fully utilize the constitutional tools we were given and expected to use.

Dissatisfaction with the rate of legislative progress and responses to the growing list of problems we have has begun to increase while Congress passes fewer laws and is perceived as less effective. Elected officials are expected to represent the wishes of the people, not a lobby or special interest group, and to make changes in governance and laws. We are governed as a republic and have the ability to vote to change our leaders when we think they aren't completing those tasks. Yet we increasingly don't feel that everything is working as it should. Those of us living now have a sacred duty to pass along a better nation to the next generation. This sentiment from the days of our struggle for independence continues to have validity:

> *The Sun never shined on a cause of greater worth. 'Tis not the affair of a City, a County, a Province, or a Kingdom; but of a Continent—of at least one-eighth part of the habitable Globe. 'Tis not the concern of a day, a year, or an age; posterity are virtually involved in the contest, and will be more or less affected even to the end of time, by the proceedings now. Now is the seed-time of Continental union, faith and honour.*

> —Thomas Paine, *Common Sense*

It may have been easier for colonists to imagine a break with England than for us to imagine a break with our present legislative processes considering everything we received and have benefited from up to this time. Nonetheless, they designed a system that encouraged change. The foundation of our republic depends on the constitution they created. In order to achieve fundamental change, the Constitution must be changed. The founders of the republic purposely created amendments as the means to update the Constitution. Today is our seed-time.

We must not be timid or avoid changes to update the tools our nation uses to govern. Enabling electronic voting is a break with the past and a statement of our faith in our ability to make a different future. It is also an affirmation of the heritage and the Constitution we live under. Too often the electorate and those who govern in a republic such as ours must perceive a threat to the well-being of the nation in order to make changes of significant magnitude. The benefits we lay out here will be sufficient to build the necessary interest for an amendment. We should take our democratic future and security as seriously as we do our external security.

## How Amendments Come About

Article V of the Constitution prescribes how an amendment can become part of the Constitution. It lays out how amendments are proposed and ratified.

> *The Congress, whenever two thirds of both houses shall deem it necessary, shall propose amendments to this Constitution, or, on the application of the legislatures of two thirds of the several states, shall call a convention for proposing amendments, which, in either case, shall be valid to all intents and purposes, as part of this Constitution, when ratified by the legislatures of three fourths of the several states, or by conventions in three fourths thereof, as the one or the other mode of ratification may be proposed by the Congress...*
>
> —The Constitution of the United States

For most of our history, Congress proposed and passed by two-thirds majority vote amendments to the Constitution, which then went to the state legislatures for ratification. When three-quarters of the state legislatures ratified an amendment, it became part of the Constitution. This process has happened with seventeen amendments after the first ten, which were ratified as the Bill of Rights as part of the Constitution.

An alternative method is for state legislatures to call a National Constitutional Convention that may consider any item as part of an amendment, or to directly propose an amendment without the consent of Congress. It takes two-thirds of the states to call for the convention or to propose an amendment. These methods have never resulted in calling a convention or in proposing an amendment. Yet they were included in the constitutional plan that was bequeathed to us.

Historically, it's been easier to convince two-thirds of Congress than the thousands of state legislators to vote for a change. But whichever way an amendment is proposed, before it can become part of the Constitution it must be ratified by three-quarters of state legislatures. Some amendments, like the aforementioned ERA amendment, have been ratified by a number of states but still remain short of the three-quarters majority necessary.

Amending the Constitution is not an easy task. There have been over 11,000 proposed constitutional amendments since 1789. Every amendment finally ratified had to come through Congress. There has not been a National Constitutional Convention since the original. In short, most proposed amendments do not make it out of Congress. Fixing our government using this method will be a difficult but necessary task to fix our governance in a way that makes an impact beyond our lifetimes.

We have modified our Constitution a number of times. But we haven't used two of the three major methods given to us to do so. We're in a constitutional rut, long overdue for amendments that will update our democracy, and in part, that rut was created by unawareness of or neglect of the options we have available to us.

## An Enormous Effort to Pass an Amendment

To change our republic for the better is our goal. The first target of this book is to propose two amendments—one, to allow electronic voting and two, to retire the Electoral College in favor of voting for the president directly. Achieving these goals would require either a proposal from Congress and passage by two-thirds majority in both the House of Representatives and the Senate or a proposal from three-fourths of state legislatures to call a constitutional convention and forward any amendment to all the states, bypassing Congress entirely. The convention would determine the wording of any amendment, and the delegates would vote on any proposed amendments. Then the amendment would go before the state legislatures. Only when the amendment was ratified by three-fourths of state legislatures would the amendment become part of the Constitution. (It takes two-thirds of the legislatures of the states to call a convention, but three-quarters of the legislatures to ratify an amendment.)

Since this would be a multiyear process, by the time a convention was held we'd have a pretty good idea of how the change would work (remember, one amendment already took over two hundred years). Amendments lay out the framework for how government operates, but all the details of those operations would still have to be worked out through other legislation and guidelines. Our experience in implementing other amendments has shown that to be true.

Lastly, the decision to allow electronic voting as described earlier would impact the laws of all states and the operations of some federal agencies. If the federal government runs the electronic elections, then that wording also must be changed in the Constitution. Finally, if voting and registration are handled by the federal government, then the structure of elections in some states would also need to change.

## Prepare the New Tomorrow

JFK's admonition, "Ask not what your country can do for you; ask what you can do for your country," carries particular significance when placed in a constitutional context. The average voter does not fully appreciate the power they have over what our Constitution could potentially look like. What we can do for our country may be as simple as joining our voices to the call for change, through the constitutional process.

The average American does not need to become a constitutional law expert to understand that they hold the power to make a difference. We have been called by our founders to play this role. It is, as Kennedy said, an obligation we have.

## Conclusion

We live in a society of roughly 350 million individual channels only partially and intermittently going in the same direction. Our founders anticipated us being this diverse. But they didn't anticipate, perhaps, the degree to which we've become disconnected from our ability to make change. Today our political will only shows during election cycles, and then not always at turnout rates that impress. Hourly, there are an enormous number of opinions posted in a printed or electronic format somewhere. These are but raindrops that only promise to be a resource if they are channeled into a single river that can carve out a canyon or fill a reservoir. The authors of this book want all of us to put together our votes to influence legislators to pass amendments to the Constitution or to call a National Constitutional Convention. Don't look now, but it's about to begin raining all over the United States.

## CHAPTER 10

### We Must Enlarge the House of Representatives

• • •

*This source of corruption, alas, is inherent in the democratic system itself, and it can only be controlled, if at all, by finding ways to encourage legislators to subordinate ambition to principle.*

—James L. Buckley

Traditionally, we link democracy to ancient Greece and the life of the polis or city-state where men of voting age and status would meet regularly en masse to make group decisions about the future of the state. Earlier than Greece, primitive democracy flourished in small communities and villages when face-to-face discussions took place in the council or the decisions of a headman were supported by village elders or other cooperative modes of government. Democracy grows naturally within small groups working inward and outward to achieve common goals.

Democracy has been lightly recorded in history. In more authoritarian settings, rulers and kings could command their records and images be carved into stone or emblazoned on buildings. No one created monuments to democracy until the modern era. Yet there is still ample secondary evidence that democracy transcends nationalities and geography and is often present in human groups. One can imagine that most meetings among early democracies involved perhaps hundreds of men—most of whom probably knew each other on a first-name basis—and not millions of people, like we might encounter today in an average state filled with voters like Virginia.

The earliest record of direct democracy in Switzerland dates from 1291, starting with the Old Swiss Confederacy. It continues to this day with the *Landsgemeinde*, an assembly in a canton where mass voting takes place. Direct democracy still works in Switzerland because the population is more homogeneous than in most other countries, its mountains deterred direct invasion, and the small seed of direct democracy could grow under these conditions into a long tradition. It also remains a relatively small country. No one can underestimate the effect of time and repeated experience as a vital element for democracy to flourish. Our own democracy now has a tradition that exceeds more than two hundred years and a constitution that is intended to evolve with us so it can continue forward.

Representation can take many forms, legally or politically, but the basic premise assumes that someone who represents a group knows his or her constituents well enough to make informed decisions for them. Although in some places in ancient Greece, direct democracy took place face-to-face, democracy generally evolved into the form of a republic. There was no other good way to practice democracy when larger numbers of people were involved. Today, in representative democracy applied to very large populations, we are lucky to even catch a glimpse of someone on television who "represents" us, let alone have direct access to them to ask a question or voice a concern.

We have optimal human size ranges for groups that we recognize in a variety of settings. Many schools like to keep class sizes below thirty students for a traditional classroom experience. Some smaller schools like to highlight their low pupil-to-teacher ratios with smaller classes or seminars. Our personal vehicles generally hold no more than six or seven people, therefore showing a bias for certain family sizes. In a similar vein, communication experts suggest to us that three to six people is an optimal size for a group working on a project. Therefore, we know that there are sizes that are comfortable and conducive to human interaction and sizes that aren't so comfortable in terms of human numbers, and one important aspect of our government that should be given close scrutiny is how large the ratio of representatives to voters should be in simple human terms.

In some ways, our world has gotten smaller. The Internet and the global economy, along with enhanced travel resources, mean that remote parts of the globe are now intimately connected. On the other hand, there have never been as many humans alive as in the current moment, and everyone from poets to policemen recognize the human challenges in population growth and the impact it can have on our quality of life. Some say it has fundamentally altered the human experience.

If voters knew that they could have better access to their congressional representative, that knowledge would make government seem smaller, more responsive, and arguably more democratic. No one wants to be ignored. There is an easy way we can restore the face of representation both literally and figuratively. It is critical to the Fourth Branch that access to our representatives be restored to the more scaled human experience and that we feel and experience the connectedness to our elected officials and processes that the founders intended.

## We Need to Take a Step Back and Look at New Options

Too many of us want to be blame-throwers and lay all of our current problems at the feet of Congress. If a problem exists, there must be a cause and, by extension, someone who caused the problem in the first place. Congress in 1929 set the membership of the House of Representatives at 435. It has remained there ever since. Our large and growing population cannot be adequately represented by a congressperson representing approximately 800,000 people in most districts. The ratio of citizens to representative will continually rise except in states with declining or smaller populations. Congress in 1929 made their decision based on their assessment of America at the time. The physical size of the facility, as well as travel challenges, may have been considered a constraint. We recognize that we cannot fit many more representatives into a chamber built to the perceived needs in the middle of the nineteenth century. But other options exist, and in fact may be preferable to the current situation and offer many benefits.

The timely thing to do is to increase the number of representatives. Many political pundits have suggested that this change is overdue. Representatives could remain and work primarily in their home districts; offices would be set up in local courthouses where security already exists; plenary sessions like conventions could be held in major cities a few times a year; and Skype or video conferencing could be used for daily work. That's the way major corporations have to work today, and they are quite successful in being nimble and responsive. Spread the House of Representatives across the nation. Let the current chamber be a historic monument to the way we used to manage the republic, as we continue to use the space for historic and ceremonial gatherings. The Senate can continue to meet in the Capitol, as we discuss in the next chapter, although it too needs to be expanded.

This chart provides an accurate representation of where we are and where we are headed.

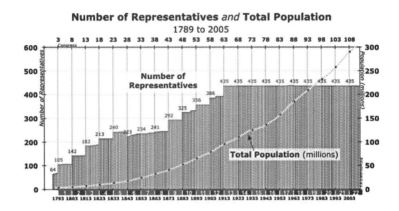

**Number of Representatives *and* Total Population**
1789 to 2005

The chart shows that the size of most congressional districts will only continue to grow. More accurately, the chart shows that the population within congressional districts has grown steadily yet that the number of representatives has failed to keep up after reaching a plateau in 1913. One can certainly draw the conclusion from the chart that the size of most congressional districts will continue to grow. There is consensus amongst many diverse experts that Congress needs to be enlarged. It will require a National Constitutional Convention to hammer out the details of the changes. We can only make suggestions and demand that the time has come to call such a meeting.

The staffs that representatives and senators now hire are the biggest they have ever been. This is in part due to the difficulty of working hundreds or even thousands of miles away from the district where a representative would normally work and live. The large staffs also help deal with the myriad special interests and other government offices that crowd inside and around the Beltway.

Connectedness, however, is arguably compromised by these variables: distance from home district, sheer number of constituents theoretically represented, larger staffs and complicated procedures, and countless distractions and lobbyists. Is it any wonder that we might elect someone and then find ourselves increasingly disconnected from that person?

## We Are Not the First to Think of This

What the size of congressional districts should be is a very large question that has always been a source of debate. The 1789 Joint Resolution of Congress proposed twelve amendments to the Constitution. Articles 3-12 became the Bill of Rights. Article 2 was finally ratified on May 7, 1992, as the Twenty-seventh Amendment that prohibited any increase or decrease to the salary for members of Congress from taking effect until the start of the next term. The other proposed amendment from 1789 states:

> *ARTICLE THE FIRST. After the first enumeration required by the first article of the Constitution, there shall be one Representative for every thirty thousand, until the number shall amount to one hundred, after which the proportion shall be so regulated by Congress, that there shall be not less than one hundred Representatives, nor less than one Representative for every forty thousand persons, until the number of Representatives shall amount to two hundred; after which the proportion shall be so regulated by Congress, that there shall not be less than two hundred Representatives, nor more than one Representative for every fifty thousand persons.*

> — National Archives

Had this item from the eighteenth century made it into the present Constitution, we would now have over six thousand representatives—a number that could be unworkable. The debate over the size of the House of Representatives was hotly discussed during the founding of the republic. Larry Sabato, Director of the Center for Politics at the University of Virginia, points out;

> *The debates over the ratification of the Constitution, as collected in the Federalist Papers and less-well-organized Anti-Federalist Papers, contain a surprising amount of discussion over the size of congressional districts (the Federalists argued that large districts were beneficial to avoid elections from turning into personality contests), and there was an implied promise contained in the ratification of the Constitution to pass an amendment regulating district size.*

Therefore, the task of resolving a proper apportionment falls to the current generation of voters to decide.

**How representation has changed over time:**

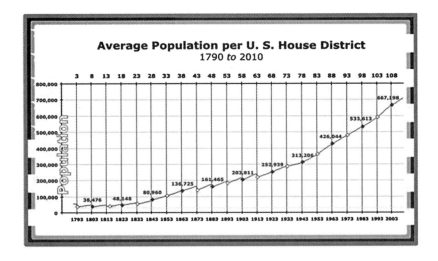

**Number of constituents per representative:**

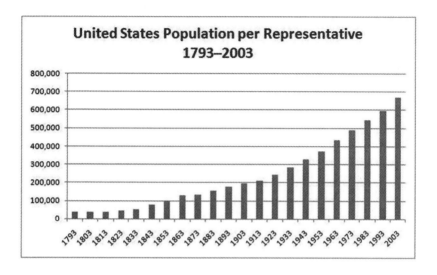

## Size Matters in Representative Government

Is Congress too small for the population of our country? Each representative in the House represents on average 733,103 people in their home district based on the U.S. population of 318.9 million in 2014. This compares to fewer than 10,000 when the republic was founded. Congressional representation needs to be expanded as a means of *reducing* the image we have of government bloat and inaccessibility by making the congressional process more accessible and democratic. How could expanding Congress *reduce* bloat and big government? Consider the fact that many members of Congress don't have time to read every bill that comes before them. Too often they must vote on laws that they haven't read or are not fully familiar with. Certainly, their staff and aides read those bills and brief them, but the truth is they have too much to do with other Beltway distractions and too many people to represent. By making Congress larger, we can actually make it work as if it's smaller.

This means in practical terms that each representative will represent about half the number of people that they represent now. We could add new members to Congress in that case, perhaps doubling the number of representatives to 850 or to as many as 1,200. With 850 representatives, each legislator would represent roughly 375,000 based on the size of a district or 265,000 if we had 1,200 legislators. The population of our nation continues to grow, so even with a reset in the size of the House of Representatives, each congressperson will represent more and more individuals. We would argue for 1,000 to 1,200 as the best size to account for future growth. The important thing is that we recognize the need for expansion.

What advantages would this have? Congress could be more responsive to localized needs, because each representative would focus on a smaller constituency except for those states that already have only one representative. Those states or territories with only one representative (some of them non-voting) are Alaska, American Samoa, Delaware, District of Columbia, Montana, North Dakota, Northern Mariana Islands, Puerto Rico, South Dakota, Vermont, Virgin Islands, and Wyoming. Depending on their population, this change could give some of these states and territories additional representatives. Most major metropolitan areas consist of at least one million people or more, so this could enable a congressperson to represent contiguous neighborhoods again, rather than entire cities or regions. It would bring government back to smaller cities and rural areas that are now sorely underrepresented due to urban sprawl and to redistricting that doesn't take into account natural neighborhoods and regions.

A larger House of Representatives also means that the opportunity to break gridlock might finally be feasible. By expanding Congress and letting them meet virtually most of the time, our democracy could return to the days when your representative could be literally someone you knew, a neighbor or a business partner. Changes to the Constitution around the number of representatives could limit gerrymandering by keeping districts contained and smaller. No more Rorschach-looking districts. Expanding the House also acknowledges that the world is a bigger place than it has ever been before. In a village of 100, there literally is no stranger; in a town of 10,000, practically everyone knows everyone; in a city of 100,000, still a small town, separations increase; in a city of 1,000,000, suddenly the dynamic is different— crime is anonymous; demographic patterns are harder to influence; schools provide uneven access and face more problems; and overall social problems are more complicated and diverse. In a nation of tens of millions, it is likely that many people from a national perspective may feel disconnected from their federal government. Who currently communicates directly with a congressperson? The complaints about Congress are at an all-time high. Legislators have the same level of skill that they have always had, but the real disconnection—the largeness of everything—has in fact become the primary problem. Wouldn't it be ironic, indeed, if we are blaming the politicians and it is actually this other factor that is the problem?

Our representative democracy should, as the Founding Fathers intended, be one of the most responsive and relevant institutions in our lives. It should be the first rather than the last to respond. And it definitely should not be taking rear-guard action, as we need to move forward. Our ability to even comprehend how many "neighbors" we have is reflected in the current disconnection and disassociation many Americans feel with Congress. The connections we create with Facebook, Twitter, and Tumblr are scattered and stratified, but they demonstrate the tools we have to connect. In the land of laws, we must connect in more structured ways and utilize all of the means available to us to make our democracy as responsive as it can be.

## The Ultimately Inescapable Solution Stares Us in the Face

Our Constitution is a living document, meaning that it was intended to be changed. What better time than in the present? As we've discussed through this book, we are overdue for change. An amendment that adapts our system to how we live now and how we need to solve problems now is the perfect example of an amendment that the Founding Fathers would have found highly appropriate. Therefore, we are arguing for a constitutional amendment that specifically expands the House by adding to the total number of representatives. For the sake of argument, we assume we would triple the size of the House of Representatives to 1,200 as a discussion point.

Along with that expansion, other commonsense changes would facilitate a return to more democratic representation. For example, representatives would spend no less than 50 percent of their allotted job time in their home districts. Congress would conduct most of its work virtually by utilizing current and future communications technologies. Rural representatives could use Skype to talk to individual constituents or small groups. This is already the world we live in, and it needs to become the world our representatives work in.

## How It Would Work

Critics might suggest that this will violate our long traditions, cost money, wreck the multibillion dollar industries that have grown up around "status quo" government and the Beltway, and create social unrest. These arguments can each be debunked. We possess a fine and noble tradition, with several hundred years of remarkable history. But we have also made mistakes, and to correct them we changed the Constitution. We did this to end slavery and to limit the terms of the office of president. Tradition cannot be a reason to leave a broken system in its broken state. By law, for instance, when the tread on your tires goes below a certain level, your vehicle will no longer pass inspection. Does our political system still pass inspection?

The answer is no. Failing to take action around a known deteriorating condition is irresponsible. In the case of the car and the tires, the owner would be liable. Ignoring the problem can mask the fear of change. Our tradition, however, has been to embrace change through constitutional amendments. If we don't change our Constitution and adapt, we are in fact violating our tradition. Tradition is not a good reason to keep Congress the size that it is.

Several multibillion dollar industries have grown up around politics in Washington, D.C. and many believe that they smother aspects of democracy. These current campaign-connected processes and manipulations will not easily be dismantled. Resistance to an expanded House will be fierce among everyone who stands to lose their benefits and political influence based on money and power. This will no doubt be the most difficult obstacle, but it is one that everyone outside the Beltway knows needs to be overcome. Voters will hear messages and appeals more closely aligned with the average person's goals.

The possibility of social unrest is always present in all forms of government. Democracy encourages a free press, freedom to assemble, and the right to voice an opinion. Expanding the House could reduce social unrest, rather than promote it, since voters will feel more connected to those running for the new House of Representatives. Voters can request an appointment with their representative and drive to their office in one day from wherever voters live. If things stay as they currently are, disenchantment, discouragement, and anger are likely to increase. Gridlock and partisanship are not antidotes to social unrest—they encourage it.

## Summary

All in all, there are too many reasons why this is the right time, and the right place. It's time to expand Congress. Why are we waiting? We do not expect every idea to be embraced, especially those ideas that are simply not workable. But we all have some skin in the Fourth Branch game. Detailing all the problems to be solved goes on minute-by-minute on the news channels and many, many blogs. That's great. But we need to agree to sit down together and determine what solutions we can craft on our own, with the tools the founders gave us. Expecting solutions from Washington simply by waiting seems unlikely to achieve the goals we seek. Any change will take time, which we argue we are running out of. How hard is it to vote to change something? How much risk is there to calling a National Constitutional Convention to look at potential solutions?

Just because there is fear of change does not mean that we shouldn't make an effort to improve the current situation. It might mean building a larger structure for an enlarged Congress to meet in. It might mean having Congress meet somewhere outside the Beltway. It might mean more virtual meetings. But it is not written anywhere in the Constitution that the House of Representatives must remain exactly how it is. We can fund a prototype to allow a small number of current representatives to work from their home districts before we look at changing the Constitution. Imagine if it does work and plenary sessions could take place in St. Louis, Milwaukee, Birmingham, or Salt Lake City—then voters and schoolchildren could actually witness laws being made on the floor of a convention center. Would they not feel closer to their government?

# CHAPTER 11

## Enlarging and Reforming the Senate

• • •

*The reason that minorities and women don't have a better shot at getting elected to the Senate or to statewide office is because the campaign finance rules are so skewed as to make it very difficult for non-traditional candidates to raise the money necessary to get elected.*

—Carol Moseley Braun

On July 17, 1787, the framers of the Constitution determined via the Great Compromise to establish a bicameral legislative body for the new nation. States would receive equal representation in the Senate while representation based on population would drive membership in the House of Representatives. They crafted the Senate to serve as a counterweight to the potential brute force of simple majority rule.

### Background

The purpose of the War of Independence from Britain in 1776 was simply to throw off the yoke of royal rule and let each colony achieve independence. No fully defined American nation existed at the end of the war in 1781. Representatives of George III of England and representatives of the Congress of the Confederation plus other nations that also aligned against the British on September 3, 1783 signed the Peace of Paris ending the War of Independence. During that time, communications and travel did not happen quickly and no evening news tried to interview all of the parties involved. The thirteen original colonies had created a Continental Congress for the purpose of conducting war with little further thought about what would follow. No one knew for sure we could win independence from the strongest nation on the planet in 1776, so it was natural to take it one step at a time. All during this period, the political situation was very fluid, to say the least. Capture and hanging for the Founding Fathers was a genuine possibility during those years.

After peace with Britain, still no American nation yet existed. The closest we came was in references in both *Common Sense* by Thomas Paine and *The Declaration of Independence* to the entity of "America." Paine refers once to "free and independent States of America" in his pamphlet. Only the Articles of Confederation held the states together, even at the conclusion of the Peace of Paris. The articles could be described as sufficient for directing the war effort but not strong enough to create a nation. In the 1780s, the average person's world was very small. No one gave much thought to governance or even if government at any level beyond an independent state was needed. At the conclusion of the War of Independence, there was no republic, no nation, and no true democracy. Joseph J. Ellis, a leading scholar of American history and winner of the Pulitzer Prize for History, says the mindset at that time among our leaders was not antidemocratic but "predemocratic." No adequate way exists for us to grasp the difference in those times and our times. Some might wish to go back to times of no government, but that is no longer a path open to us either.

Most of the newly independent colonists obviously did not want a king for their new government. Although they were used to the leadership of royal governors, they were also skeptical of the amount of authority vested in those offices. When they eventually began conversations about how to create a representative government, the roles for representatives and senators would be informed by this historical perspective.

Beginning in 1774, the thirteen colonies formed a Continental Congress for the purpose of securing independence from Britain. The product of those early sessions of the Second Continental Congress was the adoption of the Declaration of Independence on July 4, 1776. At the top of the document, Jefferson and the Continental Congress refer to Thirteen United States of America. The United States at that time was more a geographical entity than a nation as we think of nations today. In order to conduct war, the Articles of Confederation served as a pseudo constitution. The powers of the Continental

Congress under the articles remained weak. George Washington, serving as commander of the Continental Army, constantly wrote to the Continental Congress to raise money to pay the army and provide much-needed supplies. Because the articles were weak, Congress did the best it could to fund the war. To this day, it remains a miracle that we came into existence. Washington was like a character in a horror film we've all seen. There was a knife-wielding Redcoat at the front door, and there was no phone and no way out. That the film ended the way it did, with the villain slain, was not an assured outcome. Now we must keep the miracle of democracy going the way a magician keeps plates spinning at the top of a stick.

After the war ended, times got very interesting for the Continental Congress. Under the Articles of Confederation, there was no true central government, no executive or judicial branches. There was little if any differentiation amongst the roles of those elected to the congress. The government did not coin money, tax citizens, regulate trade, or have a military. It was up to each state to manage these things separately. Congress had to request funds from the states to pay the war debt. By 1787, it was apparent the new country needed a stronger form of central government and a legislature with more nuanced roles for legislators. The country was bankrupt, having no treasury and extensive war debts; it had no centralized military and was open to attack; and there was no means of settling disagreement between the states.

Out of necessity, the Constitutional Convention met in Philadelphia beginning on May 25, 1787. The delegates elected George Washington of Virginia to preside over the convention. They began discussing ways to revise the Articles of Confederation to make it stronger. Delegate Edmund Randolph, governor of Virginia, introduced the Virginia Plan on May 29, 1787. Primarily written by James Madison, the plan outlined three branches of government, with a system of checks and balances preventing abuse of power by any one branch, as well as a bicameral legislature with representation based on state population. The Virginia Plan was debated for more than two weeks, but the smaller states, fearing the loss of rights presented by a population-based legislature, wrote their own plan. William Paterson introduced the New Jersey Plan on June 15, 1787.

The New Jersey Plan was most notable for retaining an equal number of votes for each state regardless of its size and population.

Because each state had one vote, the delegates from a state had to be in agreement. Alexander Hamilton, one of three delegates from New York, was frequently overruled by the other two delegates from his state. Out of frustration, he proposed his own plan on June 18, 1787, known as the Hamilton Plan, or the British Plan, because it proposed a system of government much like Britain's. His plan was not given serious consideration, as would be expected since it had been less than a decade since America overthrew British rule.

Heated debate continued over representation in Congress. The larger states favored the Virginia Plan, the smaller states the New Jersey Plan. By the end of June, there were serious threats to dissolve the convention without a resolution. On June 29, 1787, Roger Sherman, a well-respected delegate from Connecticut, proposed the Great Compromise: two legislative houses, one with equal representation for each state and one with representation based on population. This solution, the Connecticut Plan, was ultimately adopted and the convention moved forward. The makeup of the Senate grew out of this compromise in order to get overall acceptance for the Constitution. The constituency of the nation consisted of thirteen bickering states, each jockeying for position.

As the nation grew over the next two hundred years, each new state sent two senators to Congress and representatives based on their population. As the population of the nation grew, each member of Congress represented more and more constituents, and there were an increasing number of senators. The House was finally closed off at 435 representatives, and since the admission of Hawaii, there have been exactly one hundred senators. Every decade, as the census showed population shifts, representatives have been reallocated to those states whose population is increasing and taken away from states whose population has declined. But no such reallocation occurs among members of the Senate. Our Founding Fathers could not have predicted how much our population would increase.

As a result of this, returning to our conversation about power channels, influence amongst representatives in the House has been relatively diluted over time as their numbers grew, while the influence of individual senators has become much more relatively powerful, given their unchanging status. Our founders created a system in which senators would inevitably, with population growth over time, become the most powerful elected officials outside the Oval

Office. The Senate is a key to unlocking the Fourth Branch, making constitutional amendments, and understanding how our democracy can best function.

## What Worked Then No Longer Represents This Nation

"Theoretically, if the twenty-six smallest states held together on all votes, they would control the U.S. Senate, with a total of just under 17 percent of the country's population," noted Larry Sabato, author of *A More Perfect Constitution* and a respected political commentator. He made the same case we're making, that the enormous expansion of population since the Senate began makes many constituents grossly underrepresented in the Senate. We no longer need to fear the power of populous states overruling the smaller states the way they might have in 1787. The problem that the constitutional compromise sought to fix is simply no longer relevant as a reason to keep doing what we're doing. The time for a review of the role of the Senate has arrived. What should the U.S. Senate in the twenty-first century and beyond focus on? States' rights retain value as one purpose, but that alone is no longer a strong enough reason not to enlarge the Senate. Additionally, many citizens retain a strong identification with their state, and senators serve to bring state-specific issues to the national forum.

Today, however, too much of the work of the Senate has become just to slow down legislation. That's not a bad thing in and of itself. Deliberations in the Senate provide the nation time to reflect, but there must be limits so that actions such as the approval of presidential appointees cannot languish for more than two months, or for unreasonable amounts of time (we will return to this in explaining more about the Fourth Branch). No recent harm has been inflicted on any small state by the House of Representatives due to allocation of seats by population.

## Reverence for the Senate

The Senate can be viewed as an irascible grandfather—set in his ways, but also loving. It has given us a number of despicable characters, such as Joe McCarthy, who persecuted people he claimed had links to the Communist party from 1950 to 1957 without much more than his own suspicions. But the worst senators don't leave a legacy—they leave a warning to the nation of how individuals with misguided intentions or lack of judgment can sometimes obtain power. The best senators represent the best in America and, depending on the timeframe selected, there are dozens to highlight. A current U.S. Arizona senator, John McCain, heads the list of most admired. Many former senators ran for president. The Senate over the years launched sixteen presidents. Because so many senators can have long terms in that chamber, they are able to develop and promote agendas that might not otherwise have gotten much attention, both good and bad. You could describe senators as mini-presidents of their states, having an influence at the federal level that governors do not. They are the doorkeepers of presidential appointments. It is their job to only let the best ones in to serve. Overall they have sustained that responsibility. Because the Senate is a relatively small body, a woman or African-American senator receives more attention by holding a major, visible office.

Even though Americans relocate their residences at an increasing rate, most citizens have significant ties—through jobs, family, schools, teams, and regional identity—to our states. Senators, because of longer terms of office, can have more impact and be influenced for good by those around them and reflect the nature of their states. There is much to be said for the views of a senator in their second (and beyond) terms that cannot be said of them in their first six years in that body. Great things happen in the Senate. If we enlarge it, what even greater targets can we hit?

Enlarging the Senate is not as simple as enlarging the House. Although there are many good reasons to consider doing it, there are also complications that must be addressed. Those complications go back to the issues that the founders themselves struggled with in creating the nation.

## Reasons to Enlarge the Senate

Just as we sometimes develop cataracts as we age, so too we fail to see things clearly. Our image of the Senate comes from eyes over two hundred years old. We need to reexamine our vision with a National Constitutional Convention. Changing the composition of the Senate is part of the reset of our democracy.

Just as the smaller states demanded a voice in 1787, so too do millions of citizens in Texas and California and other parts of the nation deserve a larger role in the Senate today. According to Larry Sabato in *A More Perfect Constitution*, the ratio of citizens in Delaware, the least populated state in 1787, to Virginia, then the most populous state, was 1 to 12. The least populous state today, Wyoming, compared to California, the most populous state, is 1 to 66. California, as the most populous state, holds as many citizens as the 21 least populous states combined. Within the walls of the Senate, one citizen from Wyoming equates to the value of 66 from California in terms of power channels. The 26 least populous states, with approximately 51 million inhabitants, control 52 votes in the Senate compared to the 24 most populous states, with 260 million people. If the least populous states banded together regardless of party affiliation, they would make up the majority vote in the Senate. Of course, no one expects that to happen. The framers of the Constitution could not have foreseen the logical conclusion to the Great Compromise of 1787.

It would negate the purpose of the Senate to make it purely population-driven representation, but the way the Senate works must be fairer given our changed demographics. One formula Sabato suggests is that the ten most populous states be assigned two additional senators and that the next fifteen most populous states receive one additional senator. There would be no change for the twenty-five states with smaller populations. The total membership of the Senate in this scenario would be 135 members. The complication, however, is that this move would undermine the original purpose of protecting small states; it would in essence make large states even more powerful.

Another scenario would be to add one senator to every state and create an enlarged and more responsive Senate with 150 members. The complication here is the opposite: small states would become more overrepresented than they currently are.

The scenario that we recommend would be to add thirty more senators who would be elected at-large across the nation. In effect, only ten at-large senators would be up for re-election in any election cycle. With this option, a candidate from a smaller state could be elected but these senators would not be tied to any states, thereby preserving the current ratio of senators to states, but overall benefiting the country as a whole since we would have more senators looking to national interests. This would also mean that states with more than two talented candidates for senator would have an option for both people to get elected at-large.

One other option would be to create a regional configuration of approximately equal populations and elect additional senators that way. You could then have a resident from the District of Columbia, for example, serving as a senator in their home area. The downside of this system is that gerrymandering would be a constant issue.

We believe that adding at-large Senate seats is a democratic solution and within the guidelines for change that our Constitution permits. Here again we have no easy task if we choose to change the Constitution. We could have a competition with a prize to be awarded by a committee for the best new solution. It is too easy to look to population data alone as the method for adding more senators, but that reasoning presents its own set of problems and restrictions and, as Sabato points out, creates tiers of states if some states have more senators than another. He suggests, as we've said, that the ten most populous states get two more senators and the next fifteen most populous to receive one more. His proposal would increase membership in the Senate to 135 and the District of Columbia would still have no vote; there are other plans that would have slightly different numbers but essentially make the same change.

The primary drawback for at-large senators stems from the ability of parties to get behind selected candidates and skew the composition of the new Senate to one party or another. But these things have a way of working themselves out, especially when people are ready to change and embrace the compromise that makes it possible. We know what we have and the current drawbacks. We must create a vision for a new Senate, then debate and vote for it.

We would definitely suggest restricting who could run for office in that body. No former presidents or vice-presidents could serve in the at-large seats because they could have too much influence. There will be plenty of former cabinet officers and governors to easily fill ten seats a year up for election. Wider participation in leadership could open up our nation not just to politicians but also to leaders from the armed forces, business leaders, leaders from underserved portions of the population, educators, and possibly outstanding moral leaders. Voices that would have no other way to be matched with power could help rebalance the national agenda.

If the country wants to increase the size of the Senate, as we believe it should, we will then have to begin to craft a solution. The first step is to begin the discussion around enlarging the Senate. Additionally, if we conceive of enlarging the number of legislature, we can also begin to imagine a wider path of legislative participation for the average voter.

# CHAPTER 12

## The Fourth Branch of Government—Citizen Legislators

• • •

*If I could kick the person in the pants responsible for most of your trouble, you wouldn't sit for a month.*

—Theodore Roosevelt

*The only title in our democracy superior to that of President is the title of citizen.*

—Justice Louis D. Brandeis

The first three branches of our government are well known: Congress, the president, and the Supreme Court. It may now be the time to add or formalize another branch of government that includes every voter more directly in his or her democracy. Many people don't realize that we already have a Fourth Branch—the will of the voters—because it operates inside the mechanics of our election process and has no other direct powers. In fact, the work of the Fourth Branch has become more entangled in our twenty-first-century complexity. Our founders envisioned a system where the will of the voters was never to be far away from those that govern. The way our country has grown, the way capitalism and big business have evolved and with the expanding role of the media—these and many other factors impede the will of the people, even without intentionally doing so. We got bigger, but our democracy didn't necessarily grow with us.

The recognition that we have a Fourth Branch, a more direct participation in democracy by voters, will likely reinvigorate the power of the individual, or the "Power of I," as some refer to it, within the clear intent of the founders. Not only will the needs of the people draw closer to the actual work of the other branches, but formalizing the will of the people will also increase voter participation. It is human nature to participate more readily when you see something in it for you.

The Fourth Branch can be recognized and energized on several levels, some more formal, and some more at the grassroots level and involving basic ideas. On the formal level, a more active Fourth Branch could include local committees and voting members who propose legislation to Congress and act as a partner and a check on congressional legislators. On a less formal level, a more active Fourth Branch will facilitate activism and voter participation.

If we move toward a more formal Fourth Branch, there will obviously need to be some guidelines defining who can do what. For example, we could define a voting member of the Fourth Branch as someone who must be at least twenty-five years old and have been a citizen of the United States for at least seven years, just as defined in the Constitution to be eligible to serve as a Representative. Until an individual is eligible for the Fourth Branch, they could vote in regular elections just as they can under the current system based on current voting laws.

Citizen legislators in a more formalized Fourth Branch, unlike members of Congress, are not limited in number by statute—only by the actual numbers of people who choose to qualify and actively participate. Although the powers of a more formal Fourth Branch will have to be worked out, we think some areas of governance are well suited to the Fourth Branch. Areas such as education could fall under the purview of the Fourth Branch, for example. Citizen legislators of the Fourth Branch will be empowered to deal with legislative issues that Congress either refuses to consider or historically has shown reluctance to deal with; in other words, the Fourth Branch will bring issues directly from the people to lawmakers. The Fourth Branch, due to our population growth and complexity, allows us to keep democracy vibrant and functional and works within a system of checks and balances that we are already accustomed to historically, but which now seem to be out of balance.

We inherited a great and innovative nation with a heritage, a hope, and a vision of our own worth and place in history. The Fourth Branch is about spreading our ideals, not our borders. We have now matured and grown so that as citizens we have the capability to more fully impact our governance and laws through tools like technology and mass communication. To whatever extent workable, an even greater level of participatory democracy is the natural evolution of our democratic story and the next logical development for this democratic nation.

No new buildings (except data centers, which could be combined with e-voting) are required. No politicians will be toppled or the military invoked. The time has come to enable and allow the voice of citizens to be expressed on a regular schedule on specific issues to an extent we agree is viable, sustainable, and effective for a twenty-first-century nation and democracy. George Washington wrote, "If we are afraid to trust one another under qualified powers, there is an end of the Union." He, of course, was referring to the thirteen former British colonies, but it is an apt quote to express the extension of this concept to the entire population. We only need to set it up properly for our times.

A new era has arrived that will allow us to experiment and improve on operations before adopting them completely. Before we can vote on how the Fourth Branch would work, we must set up a framework for how we expect it to operate. The next step would be to establish a series of pilot endeavors to verify a new model or models. Prototypes and testing of new systems provide feedback and promote iterative improvement for any product or new endeavor. Such testing and piloting has become the norm in the business and research worlds.

If a majority of voters believes that the path to a Fourth Branch may be a good idea, we have more than enough tools to set one up. We could create a Detroit Auto Show for potential improvements in governance. Following that we could operate smaller groups and initiatives with e-voting. Further down the road, we could actually establish voting as members of the Fourth Branch. It could be any combination of formal or informal, but just enough to provide the nation with a demonstration for how it would work on a larger scale. In a day and age where sophisticated modeling is standard organizational practice, we do ourselves a disservice by not allowing our government and democratic processes to benefit from the same. This can be piloted with initiatives that are mostly mainstream, popular ideas, such as improving infrastructure in states and regions with transportation improvements and broadband access.

Perhaps we could provide some large corporations a tax break for setting up a prototype of the Fourth Branch and enabling a large-scale test for the nation. Corporations already serve the community in ways that reach beyond business, providing services and financial donations for many worthy causes. Perhaps they could also help voters build the next generation of democratic government, too. This could turn into a new model for future lawmaking as well. For example, a test system for Healthcare.gov might have been beneficial if private corporations had built prototypes. In another vein, the many grassroots efforts to register voters would overlap a national system for e-voting.

Just as the founding of this country required a good deal of thought and discussion, the Fourth Branch and a rejuvenated American democracy will need the same. We could set up a virtual town hall to discuss these kinds of changes across the entire country. Our nation has been, in effect, a prototype of one kind of democracy. The prototype has been successful. We are ready for fuller participation now, making laws and setting priorities for our future and dealing with a much bigger and more complex nation. The will of the governed should no longer be limited solely to the ballot box every other year, but stretched and strengthened to impact both new and existing laws without having to wait for cycles of elections that are out of step with the rapid changes required in a complex, post-industrial society and economy. More direct democracy would demonstrate America's leadership again, too. Other countries committed to democracy in their own nations look to us as a more established democracy to show the way. The Fourth Branch working in concert with already established branches of government would provide an avenue for our better selves to demonstrate our true character while continuing to achieve greatness. If we set up a Fourth Branch and operate it successfully, other nations and peoples would discover another way to set up and run their countries, too.

This will be a challenging process because it involves sharing power and thinking about things differently. Democracy in American will continue to function as it is even if we do not attain the goal of a more direct democracy, but we as a nation could live much more fully and thrive as a result of such a change. This could become a thread of joy that would allow us to give twenty-first-century America the widest and deepest possibilities for truer self-governance. This change could echo for centuries to come. The Fourth Branch of government, a form of more direct democracy, will inspire us to resolve or accept our differences to move forward working together with the other branches of government. There will be no call to arms, no statues pulled down, no violence. Instead, we will transform ourselves through the Constitution, and thereby show other peoples and nations how modern, peaceful transformation could occur.

We are a unique country. Eleven days before Operation Overlord began in World War II, Lt. Thomas Meehan wrote in a letter to his wife:

> *We're fortunate in being Americans. At least we don't step on the underdog. I wonder if that's because there are no "Americans"—only a stew of immigrants—or if it's because the earth from which we exist has been so kind to us and our forefathers; or if it's because the "American" is the offspring of the logical European who hated oppression and loved freedom beyond life? Those great mountains and the tall timber; the cool deep lakes and broad rivers; the green valleys and white farmhouses; the air, the sea and wind; the plains and great cities; the smell of living—all must be the cause of it.*
>
> — from *To America* by Stephen E. Ambrose

We have an opportunity to do a great thing for ourselves and the world ultimately by establishing a form of more direct democracy and extending the democratic model. Why did democracy flourish first in this land? Some say it's because we have two oceans protecting us and neighbors who were not strong enough to overpower us. What about back in the eighteenth century? There were the French in Canada and western parts of North America. The Spanish inhabited Florida and of course the British ruled through royal governors in each colony. Still our Founding Fathers dreamed of fairness and equal representation *before* declaring independence. Something in the American experience made more direct democracy a logical outcome of our desire for self-rule and independence from before the War for Independence.

Our Founding Fathers did not declare themselves free of Britain's rule with a fully described copy of the Constitution under their arms;

their driving desire was simply to be independent from Britain. They used ideas from John Locke's philosophy with the belief that the will of the majority is the only source of true authority for civil government as the framework for the Declaration of Independence and the Constitution. But it took several years before Locke's ideals of balance among branches were debated and adopted at the end of the initial Constitutional Convention. We need to ask ourselves what changes we can make to our government today to improve it. From the signing of the Declaration of Independence to the ratification of the Constitution was a span of eleven years. Proposing, structuring, ratifying, and implementing a Fourth Branch will likely take a number of years as well. Municipal government charters could probably incorporate some level of more direct democracy within a couple of years, as some already have. Debating and ratifying state constitutional changes could take five years or more, but less time than a national transformation. We must be patient, but we must also assume the responsibility for facilitating the Fourth Branch.

Thomas Jefferson said of government, "It is the right of the People to *alter* [italics ours] or abolish it." The inability of our elected officials to define, discuss, and create solutions to the difficulties both present and likely to face us in the future demands that we establish additional methods to improve our governance. Once elected, officials sometimes focus either on their own interests or the interests of narrow constituencies. This must stop. Elected officials must be more accountable to all voters, called to their vocation to serve the highest goals and interests of unborn generations as well as those who elected them. And we, when we take our places in the Fourth Branch, will have to hold ourselves to the same standards we expect of others. E-voting and other changes facilitated by technology will help ensure that.

Many will argue that the average person could not possibly be counted on to act outside his own personal interests and will never be knowledgeable enough to participate more directly in government. Genuinely brilliant people from all across this country would love to come together to create a design for the Fourth Branch. The chatter in social media from educated and articulate Americans from all walks of life about the issues raised in this book are a clear indicator that something will happen soon. Specialists could set up tutorials and demos for adults who need training on how to interpret and weigh arguments online. We suggest a minimum age to participate, the same way our legislative and voting structure is presently organized within the Constitution. We would also suggest considering establishing minimum "standards of comprehension" in order to make sure that people are empowered to use their vote they way they intend to, although never as a means of preventing people from participating. Like a driver's test, voters would take these skills courses as many times as they needed to qualify.

The Fourth Branch is also a call for heightened general political literacy. Ideas should always be presented in ways that almost everyone will be able to grasp, so that the issues that the Fourth Branch handles will be considered wisely. With the technology available, many designs are possible to make more direct democracy work, to in essence be more universally designed. It would not replace the republic of this nation but rather supplement it, and even energize it. The endeavor and the debates that come out of it would likely lead to a national reawakening concerning how governments and laws work, similar to the religious reawakening of the nineteenth century.

In addition, we would be a better nation for the effort. The Fourth Branch could be "in session" for a short period of time when national, state, and local debates take place or it could be a virtual committee that in essence is always meeting. Issues would be juried and limited through a series of gates before the Fourth Branch considers them. The docket of the Fourth Branch wouldn't have to be limited necessarily, but would need procedures to manage its operations. The powers, rights, and duties of existing branches established by the Constitution would remain in place. For example, international relations could never be part of the workings of this body. Similarly, it should not become a means to abridge the rights of any group or individuals. The Fourth Branch could, for example, vote to dispense with Saturday mail delivery. Congress seems reluctant to dismantle anything that already exists, but this body could be the avenue for attenuating powers that may have over time grown too large.

## How It Would Work

The technology for a Fourth Branch system currently exists, similar to systems developed by financial institutions. As already mentioned, each citizen legislator would have to be at least twenty-five years of age and have been a citizen for at least seven years, the same requirements to run for Congress as stated in the Constitution. The chamber for this branch of the government would be virtual—a computer or other device connected to the Internet. Anyone who wished to participate would be required to apply and provide proof that they meet the minimum requirements, after which a person would be issued a voter card with a user name. Social Security numbers would identify a citizen legislator the first time. At that time, they would also be required to set up a unique user ID and a new password. They would have to then log in again to be certain everything was set up correctly. Anyone who does not own a computer could use a computer at a local library or government office or use voice responses over the phone; they could also use smart phone technology. Once a year when users log on, they would have to take a series of tests to demonstrate their mastery of basic competencies to be able to carry out the obligations associated with the Fourth Branch. For statistical purposes, votes would be tagged with income groups based on the voter's last tax filing. If there was no tax filing, they could not vote. It is a privilege to pay taxes in a country such as ours.

One model for the Fourth Branch could have it "in session" for only a portion of the year and it might consider bills only in one quarter of each year. There might need to be legislative managers or governors for the Fourth Branch, just as committees currently bring bills to the floor of Congress. These managers could have jurisdiction for bringing issues to the Fourth Branch plus they could propose items to be considered by the national Fourth Branch. These managers could be nominated by the president, or Congress, or even the governors of each state. Members of the Fourth Branch might then cast ballots for these managers. The board of managers would be made up of the top vote-getters from among the pool of nominees from each nominating group. For example, out of the pool of nominees from the president, the top vote-getter in that group would serve along with the top one from among those nominated by the others. There would in addition be one selected at large who received the fifth highest number of votes overall. These five would serve as the current legislative steering committee to manage the volume of issues brought to a vote. Issues that fall under the purview of the Fourth Branch would be submitted to the elected managers.

Voters in the Fourth Branch obviously have other jobs or interests and work part time as citizen legislators. The board of managers of the Fourth Branch would need to review all of the possible issues and select the most important ones. Over time, as we learn to do this better, the need for managers would be lessened. Additionally, the board of managers would work with a staff experienced in writing laws. Bottom line, only less complex bills could be handled by the Fourth Branch. A lot of details would remain to be worked out if we decide to create a Fourth Branch. The point is that we have the technology to do it.

Once managers establish the docket of issues that the Fourth Branch would consider during its legislative "session," naturally occurring forces would take over. Lobbyists, special interest groups, and other advocates for a measure would air commercials supporting their positions. Television shows would likely have panels of experts to discuss the issues, and electronic forums would spring up as well. Managers would establish the timeframe for final voting on an issue. Those who registered could cast their ballots either from their home computers or smart phones or from public computers available for this purpose.

The important part of this process, however, is that it takes place at the state, regional, and local levels. It would be direct democracy at its best, working in tandem with the branches already established.

Before casting their vote, a voter would need to pass a basic test that shows they know what a bill contains, no worse than a driving test. If they do not receive a passing score, they will be blocked for twenty-four hours, during which time they can acquaint themselves with the bill and re-take the assessments. No mechanism for absentee ballots would need to exist since qualified voters can utilize public computers and telephones and other technology. Voice-activated questions to establish access could be administered and voting tabulated by voice or touchpad or keyboard entries.

Once the voting window closes and votes are tallied, the results could be made public within minutes. Elected legislators would know quickly how their constituents voted. Bills passed by the Fourth Branch would go to Congress for a review. We could establish a rule that if a bill passed by the Fourth Branch, if not vetoed by a two-thirds vote of Congress within ninety days or amended by Congress, the bill would go to the president for signature (or veto). Some votes would directly affect the areas over which the Fourth Branch has more natural authority (unique citizen initiatives), and others would provide an indication of how a specific issue aligns with the common will of the people.

Voting could utilize a token system as mentioned for e-voting to keep voting secret or there could be rare times when we need to tally the vote by person. Legislators often have to vote by roll call and we too must be willing to say what we stand for. Lastly, quorums of minimum votes would have to be set. The board of managers might put up a bill that has little support among members of the Fourth Branch. Or the issue may need to receive wider recognition and debate. In that case, groups could rally constituents on issues there may not be widespread interest in. Here is what might transpire. At the end of the voting window, the board of managers would present the results. If the bill did not have a total vote cast that exceeds the minimum quorum established, then the bill would fail. The Fourth Branch would never be a backdoor to legislation. The president still has veto power as well.

Like any office, serving in the citizen's committee of the Fourth Branch is not meant to be permanent. It could be advantageous to limit terms in the Fourth Branch to four years. Then the voter would have to wait a year or other set amount of time before returning to that body for another four-year term. Such limitations would provide safety mechanisms to prevent any subgroup from attaining too much influence or power over time. From the start, we could randomly set the terms for each voter just as senators are assigned a "class" so that one-third of the Senate is elected every two years. The convening of the initial Fourth Branch would require voters to be divided by four and each group assigned a class of one-year, two-year, three-year, or four-year terms. This means that the total body would turn over 25 percent per year.

After the initial launch of the Fourth Branch, membership for something like the citizen's committee would be closed until the next session. At the next session, 25 percent would roll off. If no additional voters registered for the Fourth Branch (an unlikely possibility), those remaining would constitute the Fourth Branch for the next session. After one year, the first group that rolled off would be eligible to return. The reason for some restrictions would be to prevent a block of citizens with potentially special interests from "packing" the Fourth Branch. Otherwise, from the year someone registers, their term is for four years.

The great appeal of the Fourth Branch is that—being a virtual body—it can swell to as many as are qualified and willing to participate. It will require only minimal funding to maintain recordkeeping functions once a technological infrastructure is in place. This body requires neither campaign funds nor campaign headquarters. The cost to read and think through an issue is a cost borne solely by the citizen legislator. The Fourth Branch, as mentioned, may also serve to elevate ideas for laws or regulations to its partner branches. Although the Fourth Branch will be limited in items that can become law, it will be able to always propose bills to Congress and require Congress to vote up or down on any issue within six months. The Fourth Branch may respond more quickly than elected legislators on issues and ideas, especially since it will be freer of special interests. Most of all, it is open to everyone who meets the basic criteria. It will not utilize earmarks. The influence of the Fourth Branch could diminish the power of lobbyists. It will also be a way for millions of people to learn to legislate and consider initiatives and participate more directly in their democracy. The primary criticism of direct democracy is that it hamstrings elected officials' ability to govern. The Fourth Branch will actually partner with the other branches, and arguably help those in Congress work with us, rather than "for us."

It is often easier to create new institutions than to modify existing ones in some periods of our history. Creating a Fourth Branch may be easier than trying to restructure Congress, in the same way that the framers found it easier to make a new constitution rather than fix the old Articles of Confederation. The inability of the Democratic and Republican parties to cooperate spurs us to seek an alternative that can deal with future challenges like two-party partisanship more quickly. The philosophical framework for our present Constitution was formed from ideas from the seventeenth and eighteenth centuries. We live in a house constructed quite some time ago. It may need renovations, but we fear removing a timber that might be a critical structural support. But there are no hidden timbers; we know what our political house was made from. With a population of more than 300 million people, we should be able to find and appoint enough critical thinkers who can come up with the appropriate structure for a Fourth Branch. Much smaller populations, such as Scotland in the eighteenth century, produced a number of geniuses, including David Hume and Adam Smith. These men worked from an almost blank canvas without many of the societal structures of government as we now know it. We are a nation loaded with genius. New thoughts can come from anyone. Every generation is called to think for itself and to build on and improve what it inherits. Adding another layer to our democracy might seem to be a difficult task, but it is a necessary next step in the progression of modern democracy. We are simply too big and complicated to go on with "business as usual."

America needs to re-examine not only what direction we are taking, but also how best to arrive at new destinations. We need not only a map, but a plan for how to react when we reach our destination. We must follow, as an electorate, the same advice that Gen. Dwight Eisenhower wrote to Gen. George Patton on March 6, 1943: "You must not retain for one instant any man in a responsible position where you have become doubtful of his ability to do the job. This matter frequently calls for more courage than any other thing you will have to do, but I expect you to be perfectly cold-blooded about it." We will need to apply that dictum to our thinking about the Constitution. If it is not working well enough, then we need to change it.

Sometimes we may believe we are hamstrung by certain parts of the Constitution. It is a challenge to improve upon what we already have, and to change—when necessary—what no longer works to what works best for the greatest number of us. It is a challenge the founders expected us to take up. We must create a Fourth Branch of government if we do not trust that the Congress as it has worked all these years is up to the tests that lie ahead. These United States that we live in were created by an aristocratic oligarchy that we call the Founding Fathers; but it was the hard-working farmer and laborer—those who sowed, reaped, and milled grains—that did most of the fighting in the wars that have kept us together and protected democracy. Many simple, hard-working people built and rebuilt this country year after year. The same thing Lincoln said when he issued the Emancipation Proclamation applies to us now as well: "The way is plain, peaceful, generous, just—a way which, if followed, the world will forever applaud, and God must forever bless." Our nation may be functioning in a less-than-optimal way because the framework we live under has not been re-examined in over two hundred years, and we have increasingly failed to rely on the many workers and professionals who do the work that sustains us.

Congress does on one level represent the country as a whole. On another level, many congressmen and women reach Washington,

D.C. and are unable to leave behind some of their narrower interests, even those that benefit their own states. Character is what leads us to greatness and sustains the best that anyone has to offer. Of the eight presidents who owned slaves, only Washington freed his upon his death. Washington was not perfect, but he was self-effacing, and if he had acted differently, we might not have made the inestimable progress that we have so far. He might be saying now, *Improve upon what I gave you.* Washington set the example of only serving two terms as president. We as a nation broke that precedent when we elected Franklin Roosevelt to multiple terms. It might have been the right thing to do in 1940, but no one will ever know. We changed our Constitution to reflect what we think the best judgment is on that question.

What makes America such a great country is that ideas like the Fourth Branch are not only feasible but arguably a desirable extension to our existing governance. The strength of this country arises from its character. It's not capitalism and free enterprise alone that make the United States great. It's not the outward attributes that many cite about our national heritage and greatness such as a powerful military, the largest economy in the world, or the fundamental rights set forth in the Constitution and the Bill of Rights. Freedom, prosperity, democracy, and the very union of the United States represent outward aspects of our national core. That the United States is a democracy comes at least in part from the fact that for many years oceans either prevented or impeded invasion. Geography for many nations provides a defense where democracy can flourish. But it also comes from our character, expressed democratically.

The ability of America to constantly move our frontier across the continent created a precedent for "breaking the bonds of custom, offering new experiences, [and] calling out new institutions and activities" [Frederick Jackson Turner]. In short, it was a favorable set of circumstances that launched the country and set the stage for innovations that not only propelled our economy but the economies of other nations as well. But we now have new national and institutional frontiers that offer new experiences. Does any other citizenry believe in its abilities as deeply as our nation? The Fourth Branch can refocus our nation on those areas that can be improved by the more direct input of its citizens.

## Summary

Nearly every member of Congress represents an increasingly large constituency. The voice of the citizen cannot be heard like it once was. A Fourth Branch would enable a fairer representation of our nation's diversity. How can 535 individuals represent the needs, hopes, and desires of more than 300 million? The flawed way our legislators fight for their own offices and then fight to stay there hinders them from achieving our highest aspirations and dreams. They are too busy to listen. We can improve our governance, set a higher standard, and by these means tackle the challenges that face us in the future by bringing democracy back into focus through the Fourth Branch.

Formally, through citizen's committees, and informally, through greater voter participation and e-voting, the Fourth Branch represents a chance to show our innovation and willingness to preserve democracy in the twenty-first century. Although the Fourth Branch may look different depending on how it is actually created.

## CHAPTER 13

### The Lift from a Driving Dream

• • •

*The gears of poverty, ignorance, hopelessness and low self-esteem interact to create the kind of perpetual failure machine that grinds down dreams from generation to generation. We all bear the cost of keeping it running. Illiteracy is its linchpin.*

—Carl Sagan

Our politicians have visions and goals for our country or they wouldn't run for office. Every congressperson wants to put into action the agenda that they believe will best keep our nation strong and propel it forward. But if the other party does not believe in the same agenda, the honorable leaders from both parties cannot or will not engage in a sufficient degree of compromise. Recent studies show consistently that our two-party system has become more polarized that it has ever been before.

Adapted from The Rise of Partisanship and Super-Cooperators in the U.S. House of Representatives, by Clio Andris, David Lee, Marcus J. Hamilton, Mauro Martino, Christian E. Gunning, and John Armistead Selden. Published: April 21, 2015, DOI: 10.1371/journal.pone.0123507

Therefore, as citizens we take the bitter medicine over and over and yet never get well. Too often, those in Congress will not or cannot extricate themselves from bickering to actually deal with the many problems that follow them about day to day. Items that need attention pile up faster than they can be handled. We need to structure the Fourth Branch to be able to propose timely solutions in appropriate areas such as education. In cases where Congress fails to act on any proposals that languish in committee, the Fourth Branch can propose legislation directly to the president unless Congress vetoes it by two-thirds majority within sixty days. If they don't veto the bill, it proceeds to the president for signature.

In this way, many needed reforms could move forward faster. We could set clear boundaries and areas of responsibility so that if a majority of citizen voters support an idea, the idea can gather support and become a viable piece of legislation. In other words, let our ardent dreams and desires come to fruition through multiple power channels. Stephen Ambrose gave this illustration:

> *On January 4, 1971, [President] Nixon was on a televised interview with representatives from the networks. Nancy Dickerson reminded him of his 1968 campaign call for "the lift of a driving dream." He replied, "Before we can really get the lift of a driving dream, we have to get rid of some of the nightmares we inherited.... If we can get this country thinking not of how to fight a war, but how to win a peace—if we can get this country thinking of clean air, clean water, open spaces, of a welfare reform program that will provide a floor under the income of every family with children in America, a new approach to government, reform of education, reform of health, if those things begin to happen, people can think of these positive things, and then we have the lift of a driving dream. But it takes some time to get rid of the nightmares. You can't be having a driving dream when you are in the midst of a nightmare."*

By making changes to the Constitution, Americans will be able to raise their heads to discover solutions we never dreamed of before. From there we can begin to create new and innovative solutions initiated by the Fourth Branch. In fact, we may see a reinvigoration of Congress and a period of accomplishments that we haven't known for some time. It is likely that Congress would not be able to ignore all proposals by the Fourth Branch and might be spurred to action on their own.

The goals of all Americans are remarkably similar. What we lack and need is to create the framework to put in place a way to move solutions forward into action. It will not be simple or easy, but we can at least make it more likely to happen. The more power channels that converge, the more likely we can affect change.

The rest of this chapter proposes some ideas that the Fourth Branch could implement. The details of the bills the Fourth Branch could pass will have to be worked out by the departments and agencies empowered to implement them, working at the inspiration of citizen legislators. Delegates working through constitutional details in a National Constitutional Convention could define how the Fourth Branch could pass laws without first having all of the legal detail that bills currently have. In other words, citizen legislators should be proposing ideas, not creating red tape as we have seen in Congress recently. Alternatively, we could empower or elect a separate group from the Fourth Branch to write the detail of laws and present them. After all, everyone who qualifies will be a member from the Fourth Branch. How the details of a bill are ultimately handled will fall to the rules developed in convention.

If the Fourth Branch passes a bill and the president signs that bill into law, then Congress will have to fund the initiative. If Congress fails to fund it, the Fourth Branch could be granted the power to authorize the Internal Revenue Service to add on special taxes to pay for these things. If Congress continually vetoes Fourth Branch bills, or stymies initiatives, another convention may be called. If this sounds like nonsense, then just realize the incentive Congress will have to keep us from putting into action important initiatives by doing it themselves. The Fourth Branch will need to have the right to propose and pass bills that can directly become laws if the president signs them. The role of the Supreme Court would work the same way with Fourth Branch laws just as it does now with any law. The Fourth Branch will have to have teeth it can use when necessary, but hopefully few items will come its way that are difficult to resolve without working in tandem with all branches. Again, the responsibilities of the Fourth Branch will need to be worked out in discussions and working models years before coming into action.

## The Fourth Branch Could Create More Opportunities

We call our nation the nation of opportunity. Opportunity is a bus that stops in your neighborhood, opens its doors, and lets you and your neighbors get on and ride. But something has happened to the bus, or the route has changed. In case you didn't notice it, that bus no longer goes down every street. We need more opportunity buses with more stops in more neighborhoods with more ridership. We will only be able to achieve this when we can make the schedule for ourselves. Our leaders may be making the schedule, but when is the last time one of them lived where we do?

To put it another way, success is not an automatic formula. An educator giving advice to young people told them that opportunity can't be predicted. But preparation can be done systematically. Then, when opportunity does unexpectedly come up, you are ready to act. The Fourth Branch gives us the preparation and planning to react to opportunities that come up on a national level. It resembles more closely processes our founders employed.

The Fourth Branch could require compulsory national service for both those headed to Yale Law School and those headed to minimum wage jobs before they get to those destinations. Larry Sabato in his book *A More Perfect Constitution* recommends this change to the Constitution. Many others have suggested it over the years. The Fourth Branch could require something like this that cuts across every social class that acts as a leveler so that at some point in our lives we rub shoulders with those raised differently than we were or those from another part of the country.

We need to issue bootstraps to everyone so that we can at least say we gave everyone the opportunity to make something of their life. Not all will, of course, but we have to try. We must be able to go to bed at night like a stressed parent saying *I gave you, my fellow citizens, every chance.* Of course, some people we know will not show any initiative at all and just want a handout but not a hand up. Currently, our nation has erred on the side of not enough opportunities. We need to build a warehouse full of ideas and opportunities that anyone, at whatever point in life, can get advice or help when they need a job or education. We show this as an example only: each summer many churches organize teams to travel to other parts of the country to perform service for others. Suppose the Fourth Branch required some form of compulsory service. Compulsory service could be a week once in every ten years for everyone (including governors, CEOs, doctors, dentists, administrative assistants, database administrators, and members of Congress). Living in America with all of its opportunities in the twenty-first century is a privilege. If our taxes are uneven, then let's make our required service equal. No one would be exempt. The bus stops here.

Maybe compulsory service becomes part of the Constitution. Maybe the Fourth Branch creates and has charge of new agencies that work more closely to create opportunities. Below are some specific ideas. These are not necessarily the only ideas, or best ideas, but are representative of how the Fourth Branch can tackle problems through democratic processes. "If we build it, they will come." Dreams can serve as guides to specific activities, and while the Fourth Branch may seem like a dream, it could be built in ways that make it work for everyone.

## Employee Stock Ownership Plans

The Fourth Branch could focus on defining and building solutions for the nation. For example, the Fourth Branch could establish a new agency inside the federal government that would encourage employee-owned companies that have an employee stock ownership plan (ESOP). It could do more to promote ESOPs than what the Department of Labor can at present do. Employee-owned companies have managers like any other business and workers who report to those managers just like every other business. However, the owners of the firm serve as employees of the firm. The functionality is similar to owning a lot of stock in a corporation but being an employee there also. Employees in any company do not randomly decide what their individual responsibilities are. There are still management structures.

ESOPs work the same way and at the end of each year employees hold some of the capital in the company. In employee-owned businesses, the employees own the means of production—the tools, the profits or losses, the buildings and equipment, and the equity.

The difference between an employee-owned company with ESOPs and other owned companies is that all the profits go to the employees who provide the capital for the company and own it. The capital to form the ESOP could come from various sources. One way to set up an ESOP would be if the employees could put up the funds from their savings or from bank loans. Another way, employees could buy out a present owner over time by using each year's profits to gradually convert ownership over to the employees. A Bureau of ESOPs could provide tools to create more businesses where employees have a real stake in the outcome. A Bureau of ESOPs could serve as a banker or secure bankers to fund new businesses. We know of a local chain of hair salons owned by some entrepreneurs. The employees work very hard. What if there was a way that these employees could eventually purchase this chain from the founding entrepreneurs so that the profits, instead of going to the founders or heirs of the business, could over time evolve into an employee-owned business with an ESOP? Couldn't everyone win in a situation like that?

The Fourth Branch is sort of an ESOP—citizens both own and run the nation with a bigger stake in the outcome. We could put people to work and build wealth for those who would not get it any other way. We must be ambitious for ourselves and others. Special interest groups are ambitious! They lobby legislators all day long to get what they want. It is time to look at ways to set ourselves a place at the table of legislature so that our voices can give support to our priorities. It's not about taking anything away from anyone else. There is enough to go around; it's just that sometimes no one listens to us except at every two-year cycle.

## National Savings Accounts

Too many hard-working Americans get to retirement without any money at all. If someone isn't disciplined or they work for a company without a retirement plan, they will face an insurmountable challenge. The Fourth Branch could implement a required savings plan. This would be alongside any Individual Retirement Account (IRA) or defined pension plan. The first year someone works, the IRS or Social Security withholds 1 percent from the worker's gross pay, putting the funds into the worker's private account only held by the government. The next year someone works, 2 percent is withheld, and so forth, capping at 5 percent. After ten years, a person may choose to withdraw up to half of the funds. In five more years, they could withdraw up to another 50 percent. Once the worker reaches full retirement age, the money is available to them in any way they wish to use it.

The reason that the accountholder can withdraw half every five years is that some workers are so highly compensated that they will not need a lot of extra funds. Others may need the money for some other purpose. But no restrictions will be applied to these accounts. Unlike an IRA, the owner will never be required to withdraw all the money. They may pass it onto their heirs or charitable organizations.

Additionally, these accounts will be tax free. The reason for that is that these accounts will be simple savings accounts and will not soar or collapse in value, like other funds invested in stocks, for instance. Plus these funds will be available for Congress and the nation to use to invest in infrastructure. But it must be a guaranteed account like a government bond. For the working poor, this could be the only savings they may ever own. It may be cumbersome for some but is intended to help the majority of us who work for someone else.

## More Emphasis on Credit Unions and Mutual Banks

The banking system is dominated by very large money center banks. These banks operate for the benefit of their shareholders only. Taxpayers had to bail out money center banks as well as many other financial institutions involved in mortgages and mortgage securities. This was not fair. We now refer to many of these banks as too-big-to-fail banks as if they have an insurance policy backed by taxpayers that will always keep them from going under. How did we ever get to that?

The Fourth Branch could provide incentives and promote the creation of many more credit unions and mutual banks. These institutions are owned by their depositors. The depositors do not run the banks but still own them. These institutions are inherently more secure than money center banks. The Fourth Branch could provide this and other initiatives that don't take anything away from any existing bank but begin instead to create more opportunities for small depositors and small savers to have a place for their money. These institutions exist, but not in sufficient numbers, and the money center banks often dominate them due to the regulatory landscape that Congress has created.

## Ability to Tax Ourselves

Existing citizen groups buzz with ideas for other initiatives that the Fourth Branch could help to make a reality. Affordable childcare is a necessity for working parents and a key investment in the cognitive and social development of children. Rather than examine any number of statistics that show that the United States trails almost every other country in student achievement, let's just agree that as a country we need to improve our nation's education profile. Educational research shows repeatedly that early intervention, for example, is the key to helping students succeed. Because school funding is not uniform across the nation, inequality among school systems can be extreme. What solutions, what improvements, could come from working together on education when every voter has not only gone through school but also may have children in school? Maybe it's time for states' rights in the realm of education to be secondary to students' rights.

Roads and bridges everywhere need repair, but items tied to a particular region or state sometimes are harder to fund due to fierce competition for funds between the states. The Fourth Branch, on the other hand, encourages us to think in terms of merging power channels and building consensus. Congress has underfunded infrastructure for numerous cycles in spite of states asking for more. The Fourth Branch can demand funding for infrastructure, and perhaps even authorize special taxes to fund specific initiatives.

Suppose the Fourth Branch wants more early childhood education for every child. The Fourth Branch could pass the law and tax ourselves to accomplish the goal. It could be a tax structured many different ways, but it would be an additional tax on top of already existing taxes unless Congress used the opportunity to act. The Congressional Budget Office could be called upon to provide the expected cost and the new tax could be added like the tax for Medicare. Some bills coming out of the Fourth Branch could go directly to the president to be signed into law (assuming they are not vetoed by Congress).

The stars will continue to align for America. Many great ideas already exist in the minds of citizens and they require a forum where they can be heard, debated, and, if sufficiently worthwhile, implemented.

America lives in fear of taxes. We see taxes as something taken away from us. But aren't taxes money that comes back around to us anyway? The Fourth Branch could levy some taxes to be spent directly on making large swaths of the economy stronger. We can make the majority of us better off. We can grant ourselves the opportunity to discover new solutions. We could implement specific solutions in just a few cities or regions and refine how a solution works before creating a national law and rolling it out to the entire nation. The point is, we don't have to think in the circles we are currently trapped in.

## Programs for the Nation

The Fourth Branch could establish additional government-sponsored enterprises (GSE) that impact areas that typically don't get much attention. There could be one that backs people who want to set up fresh food markets in underserved neighborhoods. There could also be employee stock ownership plans instead, or the GSE could launch and back a handful of people that would grow their business into an ESOP. The intent is to create new options and to encourage power channels to flow together. Perhaps the GSE could back families who want to farm and help them get started with a grant and loans. It could be akin to what the nation did for pioneers. It takes tremendous amounts of capital to start even a small business. We need to create a mechanism to empower our fellow citizens to do so. It could be the GSE sets up local boards in areas that approve and monitor such things. We don't have to have paid government employees do everything. We can have some volunteer government operations overseen by appropriate existing agencies, but in many cases, citizen legislators can be just as effective as government technocrats.

## Closing Down Agencies and Programs—
## Sunset Opportunities

So many programs get started and then never stop. The Fourth Branch could be the branch with the power to close down programs that don't work, even agencies that simply don't provide enough benefit. For example, the United States Postal Service provides many wonderful services, but its usefulness declines every year due to changes in communications and the innovations of private businesses. Because of intense lobbying pressure, Congress may never change the post office, though it could be scaled down or sold. For communities that still need to retain those services, perhaps new ways to sustain rural pick up and delivery of mail and other items could be found. We are an inventive nation. In sparsely populated areas, Wi-Fi connections are weak or simply don't exist so there is no communication alternative in some cases. Perhaps local post offices could be privatized and a government subsidy provided so that area residents could run it without a permanent staff that requires benefits. We have to ask ourselves, if the United States Postal Service didn't exist today, what would we create to replace it and how could it be done? For many difficult problems, solutions can be found, and not every solution is like trying to catch a falling knife.

The Department of Education does a lot of wonderful work, but which of its programs are no longer cost effective? The oversight for that agency could become one of the duties of the Fourth Branch. Everyone has been to school. Members of the Fourth Branch may not be experts but could have virtual hearings around education matters and vote on what stays or goes. Also, it would give employees of the Department of Education the opportunity to suggest new programs. Teachers could start campaigns to add national programs. We won't know until we try.

The Fourth Branch could also fill gaps with programs too small for Congress to bother with. These don't all have to be agencies that need to be funded. It could be a matter of licensing and encouraging new ideas. This might lead to a Fourth Branch at the local or state level, a whole different topic than what we can cover here. Communities and groups would propose these ideas in the town hall of the Fourth Branch. The Fourth Branch could be lobbied by one (or more) of the thousands of groups working for improving conditions for a group, or even a state.

## The Fourth Branch Could Oversee the Department of the Interior

The Fourth Branch could pass the laws that impact our environment (this would have to be established by the amendments creating the Fourth Branch). Perhaps the Environmental Protection Agency could fall under the Fourth Branch. This could remove the ability of some groups from blocking environmental actions; it could also lessen the effect of politics on understanding and acting upon the science of environmental protection. This is another area for a national discussion. Nothing, friends, has to stay the way it is.

We could pass a law that requires developers to get an independent assessment of how many trees exist on a property slated for development and that requires developers to plant at least as many trees as they remove in another location—in other words, create an environment quid pro quo scenario. If you remove something vital in an area, it must be replaced somewhere else. Even local homeowners who have a tree removed could be assessed a fee that would provide the funding for a replacement tree, in another part of the country even. We need to think in new ways about the resources we own and how they can be better used to benefit us all.

## Corporate Oversight

It is a well-known fact that many corporate boards ignore shareholders and their votes. If we own shares in individual companies, and we take the time to vote, we should have some assurance that our voice actually matters. The stockholders of most companies are mutual funds that manage the money for millions of individuals either through direct investments in the mutual fund or through holdings in their retirement or IRA accounts. When there is need to change leadership or governance for a public company, there can be resistance from the board of directors or corporate executives or both. The Dodd-Frank law required that companies let investors vote on their executive pay practices. The idea, lawmakers said, was to give shareholders a chance to sound off when compensation plans are not in their best interests. Shareholders, however, often fail to vote and the outcome of the vote is non-binding anyway. The point is not to lay out all the situations that need attention. The point is that public companies need to be required to listen to shareholders. There needs to be more oversight. The Fourth Branch could serve a regulatory function as well.

The Fourth Branch could also sponsor consumer bills. Sometimes the pressure on congresspersons is too intense because large corporations provide campaign contributions. No lobbying group will be able to influence 100 million voters. Only items with incredibly wide support would make it out of the Fourth Branch anyway. Members of the Fourth Branch have many things to do besides look at issues all year long. But the most important ones would find their way to the virtual floor of the Fourth Branch and would make their way through the legislative process.

## Summary

Whatever issues and ideas come up around the Fourth Branch will generate a lot of questions and interest. These things must be pondered, sorted through, and analyzed. We will have years to propose and debate the creation of a Fourth Branch. We can test it to see if it generates enough interest. Of course, the threat of a Fourth Branch may be enough to cause a change in behavior among the political parties, thus improving the way we are governed. But if the idea is wanted, it can move forward, and it is constitutional. If it is warranted, we have enough resources at our disposal and overall talent to initiate creative solutions to the nation and the Fourth Branch. We will need to think about and assess what the powers of the Fourth Branch should be, set it up properly, and work to make it benefit America and future generations. Ideas for fighting problems that have either not been handled by Congress or that just need doing can be the focus for the Fourth Branch. The Fourth Branch could focus more on domestic issues, which would allow Congress to spend more time on issues of global impact. It's possible that Congress has too much to handle.

Again, the only action we propose is to call a National Constitutional Convention to debate and propose amendments to the Constitution that explore ways we can improve our nation's governance.

# Chapter 14

## How We Can Change the Constitution

•  •  •

*As Americans, we specialize in turning breakdowns
into breakthroughs. We don't surrender our dreams.
We get back up again—and we rebuild them.*

—Van Jones

We cannot believe that amending the Constitution and placing some real decision-making power into the hands of voters is impossible. It will be difficult but not impossible because otherwise that means we've gone as far as we can with American democracy. We also have the right granted by those who created the Constitution and then ratified it. As long as we have a vote, we have a sacred duty to use it. We can elect ourselves to offices and roles we create for ourselves. The only permission required is the permission we grant to ourselves and each other. No one believes or can prove America is finished. Yes, we have a multitude of problems to tackle. This concluding chapter is about creating the framework for the largest solution space ever dreamed of—American voters making decisions about specific issues important to them alongside the operations of the other established branches of government.

The objections and reluctance to change appear like a mountain range so tall there is no way through. There is always a pass through a mountain range to the other side; we just have to find it. No large democracy has made it this far before. We will rediscover our nation's pioneering spirit as we reimagine what our nation stands for and what it can accomplish. We cannot say to all of those that will follow us, *We lacked the will to change the things that hold us back and this was as far as we could take the republic we inherited.* We can step up from where we are at this exact moment in our history. Although we still have a one-person-one-vote nation, let's combine our votes and spread our wings like eagles to make this nation as vast democratically as it is geographically. An *improved* democracy exists beyond the current democracy. We tell our children every day they can succeed. We must tell each other as well that we, as a nation, can succeed, that we are not frozen in time with a situation like the one we're in forever. We must look afresh at our republic and respond as Lincoln encouraged us to respond in the darkest days of the republic when he said, "As our case is new, so we must think anew, and act anew."

We need to think like a producer making a movie about some perilous situation. The cast faces incredible odds, but through determination and ingenuity, they find ways to escape from all sorts of impossible situations. Success is written into the script America uses every day. Together we can write a new ending to our story—a better ending. While we might be likely to succeed over and over in millions of small ways if nothing changes, we must combine our efforts into a singular success that benefits everyone.

We can take a page from history with the planning that went into Operation Overlord for the D-Day invasion in 1944. The first step was for Franklin Roosevelt and Winston Churchill to believe the commanders they selected could invade a seemingly impregnable Europe to overthrow Hitler. We are not new to the greatest challenges man has faced. Americans with fewer resources and less technology than we have available to us have mustered the will and determination to overcome challenges like putting a man on the moon. This will be that kind of effort. We only need to figure out what an enhanced democracy looks like. We must first decide to do it and then figure out how to achieve the goals we set.

We must think like Eisenhower did leading up to and executing the Normandy invasion, planning for years before setting out. We will imagine first all the scenarios before selecting the best ways to improve the governance of our nation. Before those steps, it will take the political will of the nation to engage in a huge endeavor with the belief that the outcome is not in doubt. Our nation knew during World War II that we had to act. It is time again to act like better Americans, to stand together in a shared objective.

**What Makes and Keeps a Country Great?**

There are natural laws based on philosophy or theology that tell us instinctively whether a nation is great or not, and everyone has an opinion if you drop the name of a nation. The greatness of a nation could be a graph across time, consisting of peaks and valleys. Nations get off course, such as Germany, Italy, and Japan during the 1930s and 1940s. Looking at the long sweep of history, every nation has the equivalent of a driving record. Sometimes the offense is a misdemeanor; other times it's reckless driving. This could be another topic that we don't have time to investigate right now. We could agree on several low points of America's history, such as treatment of Native American tribes as the early settlers landed, and later when pioneers arrived in the western part of the country and settled there. Another low point was not just seventeenth-, eighteenth-, and nineteenth-century slavery, but also the discrimination that has existed after the abolition of slavery. We've had financial low points, too, such as the Great Depression of the 1930s as well as the one that continues to plague some of us since 2008. Perhaps what makes a country great is not that it solved all of its injustices and poverty, but that it tried every day to make life better for its citizens—all citizens. Great nations have great dreams.

It is worth quoting from a little book long forgotten, written by Frederick Lynch in 1914, called *What Makes a Nation Great*.

> *Surely the United States is great if democracy makes a nation great? No, for as yet she has not realized democracy. She has partially achieved it. To some degree her form of government is based upon it. The ideal is ever before her best citizens. She wears the name emblazoned upon her bosom. But real democracy has not yet been tried. If our nation can rise to it she shall be greatest of them all, and the light-bringer to the world. For all nations long for it, wait for it, and it is the ultimate political order of the world.*
>
> *But as yet we are far off. In democracy the people rule, or at least choose those to whom they*

*shall delegate that office. But in how many cities or states do the people actually rule, or say who shall rule? As this book was being written one man was calmly sitting in a restaurant in New York with a few henchmen about him picking out who should be the Democratic candidate for Mayor of one of the biggest and greatest cities in the world. There are probably 350,000 Democrats in that city. Not twenty of them have had any say who should be nominated on the Democratic ticket. This same man largely controls the Legislature in the capital of his great state, and the legislators, instead of passing the laws the people want, pass those this great boss wants, even when these laws rob the people. This boss rule exists throughout the nation. It is in smallest villages, it is in all towns, it reaches its height of power in large cities. While it lasts there is no democracy. When the United States shall have rid herself of it, she will have taken one step towards greatness.*

*Two of the most incompatible things in the world are democracy and special privilege. Yet special privilege is continually being bought from our state legislatures and from the National Congress itself. Great corporations, railroads, industries, even societies are forever buying legislation—such legislation often robbing the people of millions of dollars. In how many cities of the United States have not trolley companies, gas companies, all kinds of companies bought franchises that drained the people for generations? ... Until this whole practice of buying and granting special legislation can be stopped, democracy has not come. And the test of national greatness will be democracy in the years before us.*

*Real democracy implies economic and social justice, as well as political. Economic justice implies the opportunity to work, just wages for work done, and a fair share of the earnings produced, and certainty of food, shelter, and medical attendance to the end. We believe that hardly any one, with any love of humanity in him, any sense of the direction in which the world is moving, any prophetic instinct, will deny that this is a fair statement of true democracy.*

## The Constitution Was Designed to Be a Living Blueprint

Much of what was described above in 1914 continues today. The time for action is always today and again tomorrow and the next day after that. Created to be a framework for our republic, the Constitution was designed to be changed continuously. By keeping the Constitution unchanged, we rob it and ourselves of vital oxygen. We are suffocating democracy when we do not periodically update the Constitution. The National Archives maintains the original document behind glass in climate-controlled conditions. But the Constitution working daily among citizens requires oxygen to keep from deteriorating. The Founding Fathers may not be breathing above the ground, but they handed down a document that was meant to have life and breath. We need to get busy—busy updating the vision of what the United States of America represents and what it can still become.

In the remaining pages are specifics for creating and passing constitutional amendments. The process is difficult but can be achieved if the large number of voters who are moderates and independents decide that enough is enough and begin to join an organization that will fight for constitutional change. There's the rub, our unwillingness to put aside any personal agendas to see that we first need to update the very framework of our governance. Some of the hesitation of voters, we believe, is fear of being wrong. We somehow fear we will screw up our nation worse if we clamor for these kinds of changes. Who thinks we know better than our founders how we should be governed? Perhaps the question has to be, how bad does it need to get before we're willing to make changes? Avoiding changes to the Constitution is like turning up the heat on a pressure cooker on a stove—it's okay as long as steam can be let off, but it might explode too.

## Fears Around Change

It's difficult for our brains to reason "between" opposite belief systems. Congresspersons must feel this every day. Maybe we were born with little rooms in our brains where we store our sets of beliefs. We spend all of our time in some rooms and not others. We close and lock some doors but leave the others open. Leaving both open is hard to even comprehend. When we consider changes to our lives, we see what's in the "change" room. If the "change" room is filled with memories of failures, we quickly close and lock the door—no place for change here—and return to the "entertainment" room, where we feel more comfortable. We are creatures who seek comfort and the steadiness of knowing what to expect daily. If we change the Constitution, what are all the things that could go wrong or get worse? There is too much at stake, some might say, to risk big changes.

We suggest that we think of these changes as rolling waves of changes over years.

We believe that calling a National Constitutional Convention would be a suitable first step. There delegates could look at changes to the Constitution, such as e-voting. The convention could roll out changes we described at the beginning of the book first. We could set up e-voting if an amendment receives approval, then move on to other changes. When cleaning out the closet of the Constitution, the convention may find other items to deal with that we did not think of.

Laws must be "black and white" so police and courts can determine if a person did or did not violate a law. But *lawmaking* has to balance all the options—protect our rights while also establishing the specifics of a change in a law. It's the age-old question: do the rights of one person end when they abridge the rights of another? As citizen legislators, when the Fourth Branch gets implemented, we will need to become acquainted with how laws are made. We will engage in virtual town halls and classes that show us how to manage our governance. But first we will need to change the framework of our Constitution to allow more input on matters of governance and yet protect the freedoms granted in the Bill of Rights. Along the way we must develop the mind of America for a brighter, wider future.

It will be quite difficult for anyone to think about modifying the Constitution let alone dive down into the specifics of changes. It's worked for over two hundred years, so let's leave it alone. But the

Constitution is not some sleeping dragon that if awakened will bring havoc to the little villages of our lives and the lives of our families. Amending the Constitution will not be like signing up for a pass-fail class either. We might achieve some goals and not others. Like doctors, our first charge is to do no harm. If doctors feared new treatments, we would still be practicing medicine like we did when our nation started. We are afraid to pick up the scalpel and cut into our Constitution. We must be careful for sure and recognize our almost sacred duty when we do so. We must also rise to the challenge as surgeons often do.

### Decide If We Want to Begin the Journey

Before you go traveling to a new place, you read about it, ask others who have gone there, and watch a program about the place. Before anyone decides they are in favor of changing the Constitution, they must read it, go online with questions, watch videos, and read books about the subject. We hope our book is the beginning of a much larger discussion. The goal of such an endeavor is to understand what changing the Constitution entails.

It's like a recent commercial for almond milk. The person at the refrigerator says he doesn't want to try almond milk. He is asked why he doesn't want to try something new. He replies, "Because I don't know what it will taste like." We don't have to taste the Constitution! We don't have to digest it. We first need to get a supermajority of congresspersons to propose amendments or seek a supermajority of state legislatures to call a National Constitutional Convention. Well-informed leaders will discuss these questions. Our duty is only to make the possibility of constitutional review possible. Members of a National Constitutional Convention would have to digest the Constitution and create separate amendments to be submitted to the state legislatures.

If our collective decision is to amend the Constitution, we will have to convince our relatives, neighbors, and friends to also join us on the journey. We will then have to convince our representatives and senators to support creating the first modern National Constitutional Convention. Alternatively, Congress could pass by supermajority any or all of the changes suggested here and send them to the states for ratification. But we certainly haven't laid out those ideas in enough detail or in language that would make them suitable amendments from just these pages—they are ideas and suggestions for a large and long conversation. They need refining. We believe the best method would be the National Constitutional Convention.

## The Mechanics of Change—
## Calling a National Constitutional Convention

Article V of the Constitution is less than crystal clear about calling a National Constitutional Convention. Either Congress by two-thirds majority proposes amendments to the Constitution or two-thirds of state legislatures call a constitutional convention. We agree with Larry Sabato, a fellow Virginian and respected political analyst, that Congress will never likely be the one to propose significant constitutional reform. He says that Congress, first, by its very existence proves that the constitutional system works and, second, that because Congress has so much going on, it will never find the time, or will, to think through the ideas we have suggested. Therefore, the only way to achieve change is to convince two-thirds—thirty-four—of state legislatures to call one. It's the best chance for change there is.

Either way will be a challenge, but the first step will be to petition legislators at the state level to propose the idea and see how many states would agree to call for a National Constitutional Convention. Then statewide organizations would need to form to start gathering support for other states to do so as well. Over time, new legislators who will run on the promise to call a constitutional convention could join the vote. The key is that even a poor person still has a vote. We just need to decide to use it. Congress might even go ahead and call one if they see that eventually they will be out-voted anyway. The vote is a very effective instrument when gathered into power channels with the same intent.

## Constitutional Revision Timeline

We expect that even if millions of people support the ideas we have presented, it may require decades to accomplish the task. Our plan is to form an organization and invite other organizations to devote part of their efforts, if they see a benefit, to forming the Fourth

Branch movement. The goal is for achieving bipartisan objectives, such as retiring the Electoral College. If the Millennials, those born between 1980 and 1998, join in a movement, they would likely supply the energy required to move these ideas forward. The danger is that a movement that will require generations will simply run out of steam. It must be organized and run like a corporation, an entity not connected to any single person or group of founders but with an idea.

Many other books and websites that we have come across want to solve specific parts of problems—for example, reducing the influence of big money in political campaigns—but no organization has gone as far as suggesting that to solve our nation's problems we must first change the very framework, the Constitution, where we make decisions about laws. We hope to learn from feedback to this book and visits to the website http://www.fourthbranchofgovernment.com what the response is. We cannot detail the shape of an organization that at the moment is just an idea. As we said above, no one has a lock on all the good ideas. But everyone has to decide if any of these ideas should be explored in a fashion where they have a chance of becoming operational.

The movement that will work for constitutional change and the creation of the Fourth Branch will remain flexible shaping its objectives to the resources and demands of those that join with us. If this is the time for constitutional change, the right people and resources will come together. Once enough critical elements coalesce like a nuclear reactor, we will achieve critical mass, the tipping point, when we can begin sustained work.

The first step is to create the means of deliberation—a National Constitutional Convention. People who have never been heard from before except in protest will be able to take center stage. Our focus will be to improve our democracy and to set an example for other nations to follow for where democracy is headed. We must first buy the land, plow the field, and plant the seeds before we can begin the harvest.

# Epilogue

The ideas presented here are meant to be a starting point. Quite obviously, we need a broad and wide-ranging national discussion before beginning to modify the Constitution. Our conclusion simply says that to change the Constitution in a meaningful manner will require calling for a National Constitutional Convention, something that has been done only once for the purpose of replacing the Articles of Confederation with the present Constitution. We advocate changing the framework of the Constitution so that, as a nation, we can make our laws differently within an expanded, more far-reaching and more direct democracy. Specific items listed in any of the chapters are meant to be examples of laws that could come out of an expanded framework. Amendments that should be laws have no place in the Constitution. Just to call a National Constitutional Convention will be multi-step process.

The Constitution does not list specific steps or procedures for holding a National Constitutional Convention. To even begin will require effort and cooperation from Congress, the Executive Branch, the Supreme Court, and state legislatures. As already mentioned, we will need to create a Manhattan Project for constitutional changes. We will need not only the government, but also individuals, universities, and foundations, as well as leaders from the business community. It will require a two-phase effort: one to figure out how to set up and conduct a constitutional convention and a second phase to structure and vote on proposals coming out of a National Constitutional Convention. The reason to expend as much effort as this process will take is because it is necessary to permanently establish a methodology and legal structure to conduct constitutional conventions for future generations.

Here's what the Constitution says in Article 5 about amendments to the Constitution :

*The Congress, whenever two thirds of both
Houses shall deem it necessary, shall propose
Amendments to this Constitution, or, on the
Application of the Legislatures of two thirds of the
several States, shall call a Convention for proposing
Amendments, which, in either Case, shall be valid to
all Intents and Purposes, as part of this Constitution,
when ratified by the Legislatures of three fourths of
the several States, or by Conventions in three fourths
thereof, as the one or the other Mode of Ratification
may be proposed by the Congress; Provided that no
Amendment which may be made prior to the Year
One thousand eight hundred and eight shall in any
Manner affect the first and fourth Clauses in the
Ninth Section of the first Article; and that no State,
without its Consent, shall be deprived of its equal
Suffrage in the Senate.*

What the framers said was, *put to a vote changes to the
Constitution when two thirds of Congress or state legislatures want
to propose a change and if three fourths of the legislatures go along
with it, then make those amendments.* We believe they thought we'd
be smart enough to figure out how to do it. We are not only smart
enough to do it, but the faith of the founders mean we need to be brave
enough to make it happen.

In theory, Congress could write as many amendments as are needed
to cover all the basic changes laid out in this book, but adding that
workload to Congress and securing the votes to pass the amendments
to the states for ratification could take a long time. The number of
proposals that have made it out of Congress as amendments in the last
fifty years indicates that Congress is not up to the task. Like a football
game, we must go long!

There are enough legal scholars within foundations, government,
courts, and universities who could figure out how to accomplish the
task of setting up and conducting a constitutional convention. Their
findings could be presented to Congress or state legislatures to serve
as instructions to a new National Constitutional Convention. Their
findings could also be codified as an amendment and permanently
settle how to convene a constitutional convention. The challenges we

face now and will face in the future are significant enough to require us to settle how to update our Constitution. Many states have already set up procedures for constitutional conventions. Perhaps one of these, or the best of several, could be adapted at the national level.

One of the outcomes from this process could be the restoration of civility in our governance. The mission of the Fourth Branch must establish a framework (implicit or explicit) of kindness. When we argue with a friend we continue to treat our friend with kindness. Deliberations and forums of the Fourth Branch will be filtered not only for slander and hate but for angry words as well. Over time, we can re-establish our democracy on a foundation of courtesy if not outright kindness. Laws must benefit society not any group. The Fourth Branch of Government could be like fitting our nation with a new pair of glasses to enable enhanced vision to future possibilities.

### We First Need to Determine If We Want Change

Hopefully, some corporations and foundations will combine resources to create an electronic town hall where ideas can be put forth and refined and where informal votes can be conducted to determine if the support exists for various changes like those we propose. This would also serve as the first prototype of the Fourth Branch where ordinary citizens debate and vote. Doing this would not require any major changes. With the future of so many others beyond this generation at stake, surely we can discover some ways to begin the conversation about changes that need to be made.

### How Many Voters Are Necessary For Change?

What if polls showed a majority of voters wanted constitutional change but not a supermajority (67 percent)? The supermajority requirement only applies to congressional votes and the total votes of state legislatures. In other words, a simple majority in most cases could assure changes to the Constitution at most levels. Each state has its own rules for ratifying amendments to the United States Constitution. It may be that making changes to the Constitution could be carried out more easily at the state level than going through Congress, but that is a separate subject beyond the scope of our present book. We simply want to raise awareness. We have tools at our disposal.

What if Congress and/or state legislatures, as a whole, are unwilling to take the steps needed? We would have two choices. Many legislators at both the state and national levels likely favor some changes to the Constitution, as is increasingly evident from media reports. But to reach the majority and supermajorities required would mean some new legislators would need to be elected. The first step to changing the complexion of an electoral body would be to elect candidates willing to convene a National Constitutional Convention. The second, more difficult, way would be to create a National Constitutional Convention Party that would put forth their candidates in opposition to the current national parties. This would likely not work at the national level, but might work at the state level. Either option would require individual voters in favor of a constitutional convention to come off the sidelines and vote in very large numbers. It may likely be that we need to create a grassroots organization for the sole purpose of calling a National Constitutional Convention. We will only know with time.

Please do not remain silent on these matters. We believe, friends, that the juice is worth the squeeze.

# Fourth Branch Discussion Questions

1.  How much or how often do you think our founders intended for the Constitution to be updated? What kind of history were you taught about this when you were young?

2.  What do you think functions well in our democracy right now? What is the most broken aspect of it?

3.  When someone invokes the Constitution, what is the first thing you think?

4.  How do we bring about change if the people in power are resistant to change?

5.  Does your vote matter? Why or why not?

6.  If you could vote using smart technology, would you do that rather than travel to the polls to vote in person?

7.  Is Congress doing its job? What makes you think that?

8.  What do your friends and family think about what is being done by Congress and state legislatures to increase or sustain economic opportunities for them?

9.  Is there enough broad support for changing the Constitution among voters or must we wait until elected officials take action?

10. Do you think you and your friends and relatives know enough to vote properly for the kinds of changes suggested by this book?

11. In your heart of hearts, do you think we, as a nation, have the guts to make hard changes if they are required?

12. Can we find, or build, a moderate, middle-of-the-road, path that we can all follow?

13. Can economic inequality be reduced? Should it be reduced? Does it matter?

14. If you believe we need to make a more level playing field for our citizens, is the Constitution the place to do it?

15. Would some form of compulsory service be good for the nation? For young people? For all citizens? Could it be part of the path to citizenship?

16. Would the discussion leading to calling a National Constitutional Convention improve our nation? Why? Why not?

# ABOUT THE AUTHORS

GUY TERRELL is a project manager, as well as an accomplished writer. He earned an MBA from George Mason University, and later added an MS in Information Systems from Virginia Commonwealth University, earning a Dean's Scholar Award. Learning and writing are his passions. He has published poetry and is a past president and treasurer of the Poetry Society of Virginia (PSV). More recently he earned the Professional Project Management certification, PMP, to continue to work in technology and information systems. He has more recently turned his talents to helping American democracy flourish, thinking critically about our nation and its future.

JACK TRAMMELL is an award-winning author and poet whose credits include hundreds of articles and stories, and more than twenty books. He was a recent candidate for U.S. Congress in representative Eric Cantor's seat and has enjoyed a twenty-five-year career as an educator in the public schools and as a professor and researcher in higher education. His areas of expertise include social history, disability, education, government, American history, and creative writing. He was a long-time columnist for the Washington Times. His recent book projects include a forthcoming history of disability in America, and a recently released historical Civil War novella.